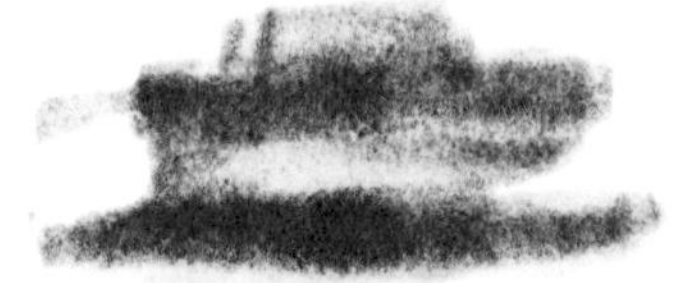

Forensic Art

Other titles in the Crime Scene Investigations series:

Blackmail and Bribery

The Case of the Green River Killer

The Case of the Zodiac Killer

Computer Hacking

The Crime Scene Photographer

Criminal Profiling

DNA Evidence

Fingerprinting

The Forensic Entomologist

Identity Theft

Kidnapping

The O.J. Simpson Murder Trial

The Oklahoma City Bombing

Poisoning

Surveillance

Tracking Serial Killers

The Unabomber

Crime Scene Investigations

Forensic Art

by Jenny MacKay

LUCENT BOOKS
A part of Gale, Cengage Learning

Detroit • New York • San Francisco • New Haven, Conn • Waterville, Maine • London

LIBRARY OF CONGRESS CATALOGING-IN-PUBLICATION DATA

MacKay, Jenny, 1978-
Forensic art / by Jenny MacKay.
p. cm. — (Crime scene investigations)
Includes bibliographical references and index.
ISBN 978-1-4205-0069-1 (hardcover)
1. Forensic sciences—Methodology—Juvenile literature. 2. Forensic anthropology—Juvenile literature. 3. Police artists—Juvenile literature. I. Title.
HV8073.M2194 2009
363.25—dc22

2008025707

Lucent Books
27500 Drake Rd.
Farmington Hills, MI 48331

ISBN-13: 978-1-4205-0069-1
ISBN-10: 1-4205-0069-4

Printed in the United States of America
1 2 3 4 5 6 7 12 11 10 09 08

Contents

Foreword 6

Introduction 8
Cracking Cases with Art

Chapter One 13
Composite Sketches

Chapter Two 29
Facial Reconstruction

Chapter Three 45
Age Progression

Chapter Four 59
Image Enhancement

Chapter Five 76
Forensic Art in Court

Notes 91

Glossary 95

For More Information 97

Index 99

Picture Credits 103

About the Author 104

Foreword

The popularity of crime scene and investigative crime shows on television has come as a surprise to many who work in the field. The main surprise is the concept that crime scene analysts are the true crime solvers, when in truth, it takes dozens of people, doing many different jobs, to solve a crime. Often, the crime scene analyst's contribution is a small one. One Minnesota forensic scientist says that the public "has gotten the wrong idea. Because I work in a lab similar to the ones on *CSI*, people seem to think I'm solving crimes left and right—just me and my microscope. They don't believe me when I tell them that it's just the investigators that are solving crimes, not me."

Crime scene analysts do have an important role to play, however. Science has rapidly added a whole new dimension to gathering and assessing evidence. Modern crime labs can match a hair of a murder suspect to one found on a murder victim, for example, or recover a latent fingerprint from a threatening letter, or use a powerful microscope to match tool marks made during the wiring of an explosive device to a tool in a suspect's possession.

Probably the most exciting of the forensic scientist's tools is DNA analysis. DNA can be found in just one drop of blood, a dribble of saliva on a toothbrush, or even the residue from a fingerprint. Some DNA analysis techniques enable scientists to tell with certainty, for example, whether a drop of blood on a suspect's shirt is that of a murder victim.

While these exciting techniques are now an essential part of many investigations, they cannot solve crimes alone. "DNA doesn't come with a name and address on it," says the Minnesota forensic scientist. "It's great if you have someone in custody to match the sample to, but otherwise, it doesn't help. That's the investigator's job. We can have all the great DNA evidence in the world, and without a suspect, it will just sit on a shelf. We've all seen cases with very little forensic evidence get solved by the resourcefulness of a detective."

While forensic specialists get the most media attention today, the work of detectives still forms the core of most criminal investigations. Their job, in many ways, has changed little over the years. Most cases are still solved through the persistence and determination of a criminal detective whose work may be anything but glamorous. Many cases require routine, even mind-numbing tasks. After the July 2005 bombings in London, for example, police officers sat in front of video players watching thousands of hours of closed-circuit television tape from security cameras throughout the city, and as a result were able to get the first images of the bombers.

The Lucent Books Crime Scene Investigations series explores the variety of ways crimes are solved. Titles cover particular crimes such as murder, specific cases such as the killing of three civil rights workers in Mississippi, or the role specialists such as medical examiners play in solving crimes. Each title in the series demonstrates the ways a crime may be solved, from the various applications of forensic science and technology to the reasoning of investigators. Sidebars examine both the limits and possibilities of the new technologies and present crime statistics, career information, and step-by-step explanations of scientific and legal processes.

The Crime Scene Investigations series strives to be both informative and realistic about how members of law enforcement—criminal investigators, forensic scientists, and others—solve crimes, for it is essential that student researchers understand that crime solving is rarely quick or easy. Many factors—from a detective's dogged pursuit of one tenuous lead to a suspect's careless mistakes to sheer luck to complex calculations computed in the lab—are all part of crime solving today.

Cracking Cases with Art

Human beings have a remarkable ability to recognize each other. Based on nothing more than the shape of someone's face, people recall names and facts about that person. The human brain files away thousands of virtual folders in its memory banks, one for each person it knows. This is how family and friends can tell each other apart from strangers, and it is why school yearbooks are popular—people can page through hundreds of faces, even years after graduating, and name friends they have not seen in a very long time. Aged faces from that high school yearbook will still spark a memory at a class reunion twenty years later, despite baldness, weight gain, wrinkles, or eyeglasses.

This human ability to store faces in memory has long interested law enforcement departments. Criminals often get away from the scene of their crime, but not always before someone sees them. An eyewitness could provide an important clue that will help investigators solve a case. Early attempts to identify criminals from eyewitness testimony, in fact, led to some of the first composite sketches, or drawings of a suspect based on how the witness told the artist the person looked.

One of the earliest examples of a composite sketch was a drawing of the notorious London killer Jack the Ripper. This portrait, which was based on the memory of someone who claimed to have seen the sneaky slayer, was printed in the newspapers of the time. It brought no new leads in the case, possibly because there were no guidelines back then for making effective composite sketches. Also, the Ripper killed only at night, and since there were no streetlights in the 1800s, it is likely that the witness's view of the person was not very good.

THE PENNY ILLUSTRATED PAPER
AND ILLUSTRATED TIMES

KATE EDDOWES THE MITRE SQUARE VICTIM

SKETCH OF THE MAN WHO VISITED MR LUSK

A sketch of a man suspected of being Jack the Ripper—one of the earliest examples of forensic art—is featured in a London newspaper in October 1888, alongside a portrait of one of his victims, whom a witness claimed the man visited shortly before her death.

Still, the idea that the public could help spot crooks through the use of composite sketches caught on quickly. In the late 1800s, French anthropologist Alphonse Bertillon tried to make the process of drawing criminals' faces scientific. He believed every face had specific, measurable differences, and the exact facial measurements of any criminal would be different from all others. His process of face measurement seemed to work well until a case came up that involved two men who, although they were unrelated, looked almost exactly alike and had the same facial measurements. Ironically, they even had the same name: William West. But only one man was guilty of the crime. Fortunately, police had knowledge of

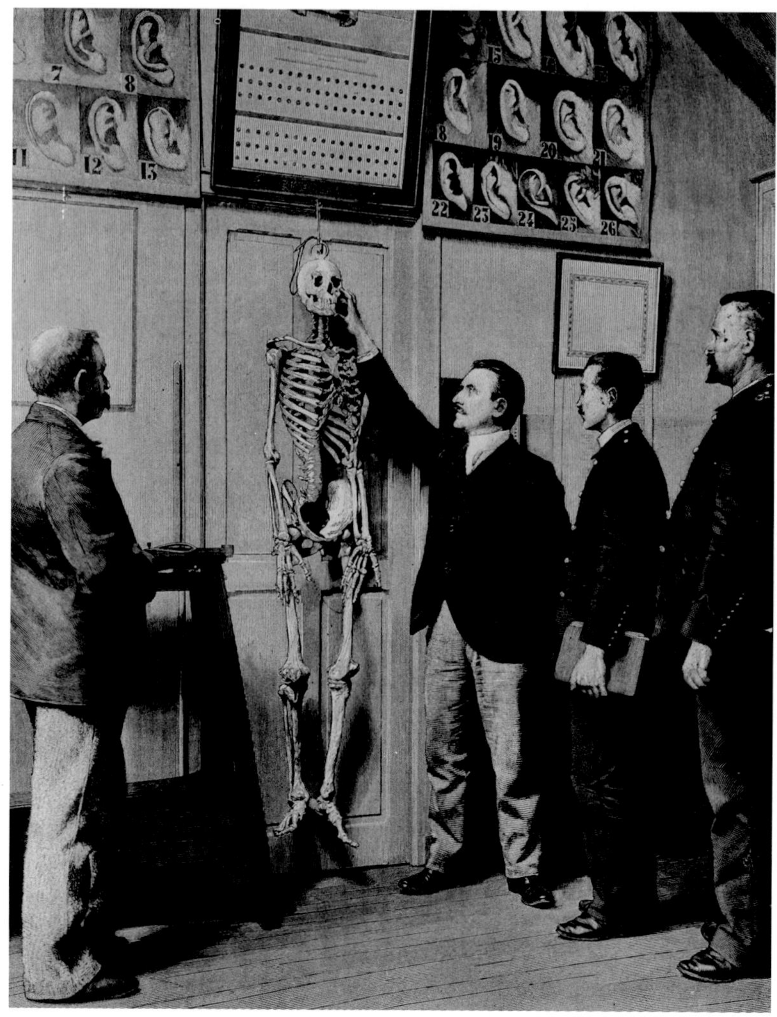

In an 1899 photograph, French anthropologist Alphonse Bertillon demonstrates his method of determining identity through the measurement of specific features and body parts, which are unique to each person.

fingerprints by then and were able to prove which William West was guilty.

Identifying people from faces alone is not as precise as most courts of law would prefer. Unlike fingerprints and DNA, both of which can be scientifically proven to belong to one person, composite sketches are not scientific. They depend on a witness's memory and opinion and on the artist's judgment about how best to draw what the witness claims to have seen. Courts of law prefer to deal with facts that can be proven, and composite sketches leave a lot of potential doubt as to whether the person in the drawing actually looks like the person who committed the crime.

Despite the fact that it is not always useful in court, forensic art has a long history in fighting crime, dating back to the Jack the Ripper sketch and the "Wanted: Dead or Alive" posters that once peppered the American West. Forensic art often gives police useful tips in the search for suspects and may help them narrow down their suspect list to the person who committed the crime.

Police departments often use composite sketches to find new leads in tough cases. They also call in artists to sculpt faces back onto skulls of unknown victims, giving them a good idea of what the person might have looked like and assisting them in their search for the victim's identity. Artists can even use old photos and a process called age progression to create pictures of how fugitives or missing persons from cases long ago might look today. These techniques have helped police to track down suspects and kidnapped persons and to identify murder victims even decades after their disappearance or death.

Advances in photography and digital technology make some aspects of forensic art, such as age progression of photographs, easier and more accurate. Photographs also turn up more often than ever before as evidence of crime. Photo-snapping cell phones and pocket-size digital cameras have become so common that witnesses to crimes often have a camera in hand to take pictures of the event. A modern-day Jack the Ripper might have more than just eyewitness testimony haunting him—the image of his face could be locked in a witness's iPhone. To retrieve and enhance this photographic evidence, police may turn to image experts, photography professionals who specialize in retrieving and clarifying images captured on film and in digital files.

Whether they sketch composites, sculpt facial reconstructions, conduct age progression of old photos, or sharpen blurry images, forensic artists usually are not police officers but professional artists who work as paid consultants, lending their creative talents to the forensic team to solve crime. They can give police departments a good lead in unsolved cases, both new and old, but the job is not easy. Although most forensic artists are well trained both in art and in police procedure, they often have to work hard to prove themselves to police departments that may be skeptical about the effectiveness of forensic sketches. There is no guarantee that their work will ever lead to the capture of a criminal or the identification of a victim, and they may be ridiculed for creating a finished product that looks very little like the person it is supposed to resemble. Still, when an artist's image of a victim or suspect shows up on the six o'clock news, it sometimes generates tips that help police solve the crime, and this is the reward forensic artists receive from the hard work they do.

With their work, forensic artists give police possible leads. It is up to investigators to take the information and clues forensic artists provide and use these to narrow down a list of suspects or unidentified victims. Proof of any suspect's guilt or innocence does not lie in the forensic artist's tool kit, but a crucial start to the investigation of a difficult case might.

Composite Sketches

The only thing more frustrating for police departments than an unsolved crime is an unsolved crime with no leads. Sometimes, the only evidence is the memory of a witness. What the witness says about what happened and who they saw can be an investigator's only clues for tracking down the criminal. Putting the details of a suspect's appearance on paper quickly, before the witness begins to forget them, is often the key to solving a case.

Working with witnesses, however, can be a challenge for forensic artists, since those who have seen a crime are often confused and emotional. A witness might be an innocent observer—one who did not even realize that a crime was committed—or a witness may know all too well what happened during the crime because he or she was the victim of it. Witnesses might be in shock over what happened to them or because a loved one or a friend was injured or killed during the crime. The forensic artist might even be visiting the witness in a hospital bed during his or her recovery from the incident.

Sometimes, a witness wants to forget that the crime ever happened. Criminal acts can be violent and disturbing, potentially causing emotional trauma even for an uninvolved eyewitness. If the witness was the victim of the crime, such as a mugging or a rape, the memory is likely to be even more disturbing, and the very last thing the witness may want to do is recall details about the frightening perpetrator. The details witnesses do remember also may be clouded by the confusion and stress they likely felt as they experienced or witnessed the event.

To do their work, forensic artists need patience and experience working with people who have been traumatized.

Hijacker, Unknown

In 1971 a man hijacked a 747 airliner over Washington State, demanded $200,000, and parachuted out of the plane in the dark, taking the money with him. It was the last anyone saw of the mysterious man wearing sunglasses and a dark business suit.

The composite sketch of a man known as D.B. Cooper, who hijacked an airplane over Washington state in 1971 and parachuted to his escape with $200,000 in ransom money, never to be heard from again, was created from the recollections of the flight's crew and passengers.

The passenger boarded the plane under the name D.B. Cooper. It is a name people have never forgotten. Investigators and treasure seekers alike have scoured the wet forests of the Pacific Northwest for decades, looking for signs of the man and the money.

Soon after the crime, an FBI agent interviewed two flight attendants and created a composite sketch. That drawing was about all investigators had to go on.

Hundreds of people have come forward over the years claiming to know (or to be) the mysterious face in the composite sketch. In 1995 a man named Duane Weber even confessed on his deathbed to being D.B. Cooper.

A forensic facial reconstruction expert compared Weber's photos to Cooper's composite sketch and found them to be a close match, but the FBI felt this was not enough to close the case. That sketch may be all we will ever know about the hijacker.

They must learn how to gently interview witnesses in order to coax accurate details about a suspect's appearance from the witness's memory. It is a forensic artist's job to get witnesses to provide these clear details, then to arrange them into a picture of a human face that other people might recognize and identify.

Sketches Bring Tips

In spring 2003 someone started setting apartment buildings on fire in Prince George's County, Maryland. During the course of the year, the arsonist set more than thirty buildings ablaze. His smoldering handiwork injured dozens of people and ruined many homes. For months, police and firefighters had no leads and no tips to help them catch the elusive person who was lighting the blazes. Then a woman came forward and said she had met the culprit. She claimed she had come home and discovered him as he prepared to set fire to her building. Investigators hoped that the woman would be able to remember what the suspect looked like so a forensic artist could make a sketch.

When forensic artists interview witnesses about facial characteristics of a person, they ask for specific details such as the color of the hair and the type of hairstyle, the color and shape of the eyes, the shape and proportion of the nose and mouth, and any particular facial expressions, such as a look of anger or surprise. The forensic artist who interviewed the Prince George's County arson witness gathered details such as these and used the witness's descriptions to draw a portrait of a middle-aged man with a medium build and salt-and-pepper-colored hair. When this sketch was shown on the evening news, the Fire Department's tip line was flooded with calls. Within twenty-four hours, dozens of tips poured in, and for the first time in months, police had leads. "It's all we have to go on at this point," a spokesman for the Fire Department told the *Washington Times*.[1]

Despite the tips it generated, the sketch itself did not ultimately lead to the arrest of the arsonist, who was finally

By the Numbers

10% TO 30%

Percentage of composite sketches that lead to a suspect's capture

apprehended two years later after leaving a pair of Marine Corps dress pants behind at one of his fires, evidence police were able to trace back to him. Although the composite sketch was not the clue that led to the arsonist's capture, the man police arrested was fifty years old and had dark hair that was turning gray, just as the sketch had depicted.

The artists who create these composite sketches are not investigators, and they do not personally solve crimes. In fact, as the arson example shows, their work may not even turn up any leads that are helpful. But because these artists draw people very well and are skilled at interviewing eyewitnesses, they are in a unique position to use their talents to assist police. When their depictions appear in news programs, in newspapers, and on flyers around a community, they usually stir up a lot of response. The tip lines may start ringing at police stations, and even a cold case can get warm again.

Most artists who use their talents to help solve crime find it very rewarding. Lois Gibson, a nationally respected forensic artist, says that artists who develop a taste for forensic drawing come to think of it as their calling. "[They] find helping investigators capture violent offenders so gratifying," she says. "They rarely care for any other kind of work thereafter."[2]

A Job Without Glory

The skills of a forensic artist are not always appreciated by the public or by other artists. Not every sketch they create helps to solve a crime, and those that do sometimes look nothing like the actual offender. The sketches that appear on the evening news are often rough and sometimes incomplete.

However, Gibson says, that is often the point. "Forensic art is the only artistic profession where the image can be poorly done, sketchy, unfinished, and otherwise flawed yet become perfect if it generates a successful outcome," she explains. "No matter how poorly a sketch from a witness comes out, if it helps identify the perpetrator depicted, it becomes a perfect work."[3]

Investigators are not looking for art they can frame, but for art that helps solve a crime. "In this line of work," Gibson says, "*catching the criminal* is more important than work that *looks good*."[4] In fact, less is often more when it comes to forensic sketching. A picture that people are told looks kind of like a suspect may bring in more calls than a picture that is said to look exactly like a suspect. A forensic artist may, therefore, create a vague picture on purpose.

A sketch of a suspect in an assault case hangs among other postings on a college campus bulletin board with the hope that someone who sees it will connect the likeness to a real person and help solve a crime.

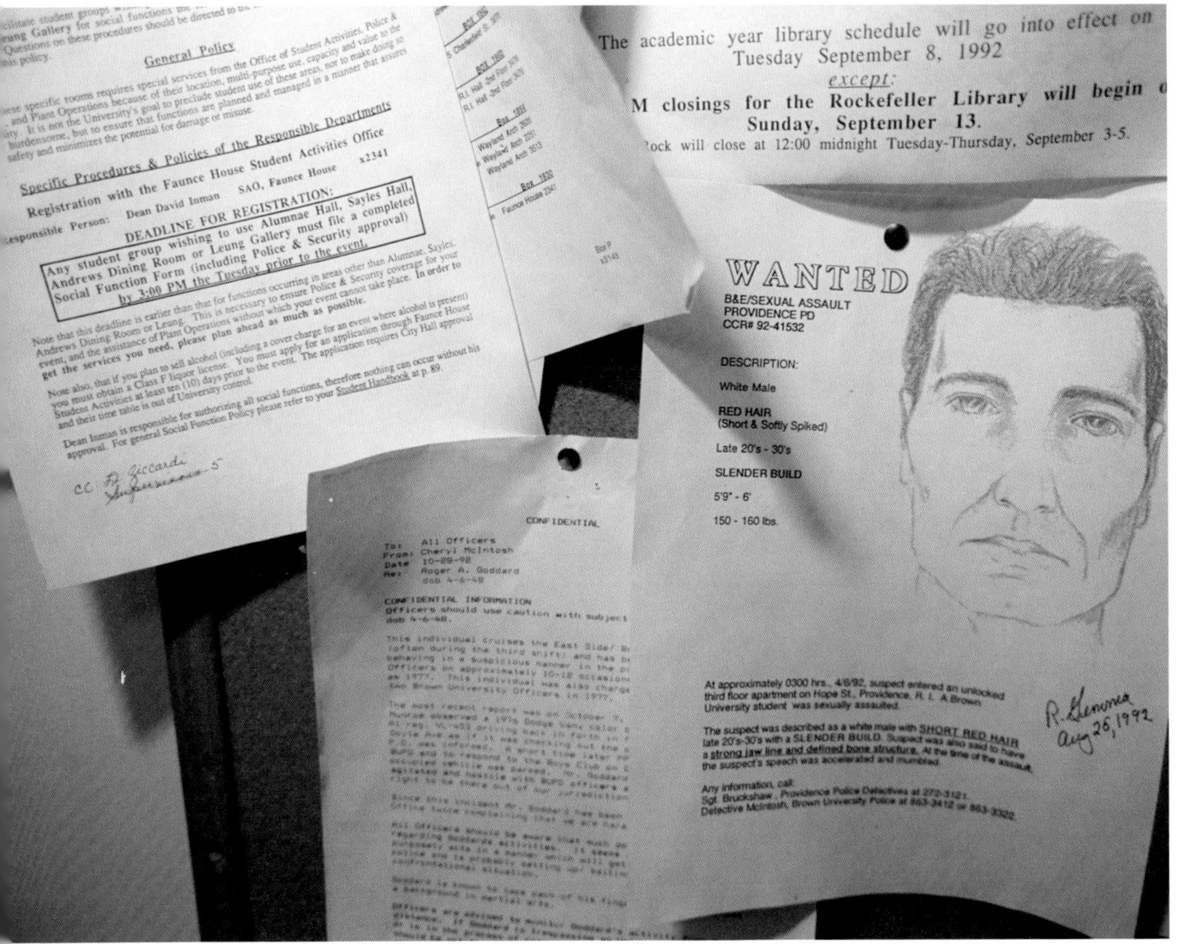

Becoming a Forensic Artist

Job Description:
Forensic artists are called on to perform many tasks. They composite sketches of suspects, sculpt or sketch facial reconstructions, create age progressions of missing persons, and sketch crime scenes. Some specialize in just one task, such as sculpting facial reconstructions, while others perform all tasks.

Education:
An associate's degree in a technical or artistic field is the minimum requirement. Many forensic artists take classes in biology, psychology, or anthropology in addition to formal training in art, and they may also need training in computer programs used for sketches and facial reconstruction.

Qualifications:
Forensic artists can become certified through the International Association for Identification. This requires eighty hours of approved coursework, one year of work experience, and twenty-five composite drawings, two of which have to successfully lead to the identification of a suspect.

Additional Information:
Many forensic artists are freelancers who develop their own list of clients. They must work well with little supervision. Excellent communication and people skills are essential, especially during witness interviews. Forensic artists may be asked to present artwork or testify in court.

Salary:
$25,000 to $50,000 or more per year

The fact that forensic art is rarely gallery-quality work does not make the finished product any less of an art form. Drawing the likeness of a suspect using only what the witness can remember and put into words is extremely hard to do, no matter how well the artist can draw. Forensic artists cannot make assumptions about what a finished face should look like, and they do not have the freedom to add in extra details that they think would make a picture more pleasing to the eye. In creating sketches, they can use only the specific details the witness provides, putting these details in the right place and proportion on the page to the best of their ability. The forensic quality of artists' work depends as much on their skill at collecting accurate details from witnesses as it does on their ability to sketch.

Interviewing a Witness

Before a forensic artist can begin a sketch, he or she must interview a witness. There are many different kinds of witnesses. Some call the police themselves to report what they have seen. Some have been tracked down by police and might feel they are being forced to talk. Often, the witness is also the victim of a crime. Sometimes, the witness is injured in the incident. Sometimes, the witness is simply so horrified by what she has seen or experienced that she does not want to talk about it at all. "Being asked to provide accurate descriptions in such a situation must be extremely unpleasant," says pathologist Ian Hill. "Not surprisingly, the details may not always be as accurate as might be desired."[5]

Some witnesses do not realize that they are witnessing a crime or seeing a suspect, so they may not have been paying attention to details. Others may insist they do not remember what happened or who they saw well enough to describe anything. Still other witnesses speak a different language than the artist, and some are children who do not yet know enough words to describe people's faces in detail. Some witnesses may even want to protect the suspect and thus might provide false information on purpose. All of these are interviewing challenges a forensic artist might deal with in a day's work. At least half the job is the interview with the witness, and if artists cannot do this well, they will never get around to drawing a sketch.

Working Quickly

Police and the community want to see a forensic sketch as soon as possible after a crime takes place. The chance that someone will recognize a composite sketch is higher while the news of the crime is still fresh in the public's mind. So the forensic artist is urged to work fast, but the witness often requires time and patience. "The atmosphere in which the drawings are created is fraught with stress unimaginable to artists not in the profession," says Gibson. "The drawings put on public display from forensic artists . . . are done with distressed witnesses under time pressure."[6]

Sketch Pads to Touch Pads

Many artists are pencil-and-paper sorts who like the feel of a sheet of vellum under their wrist and a sturdy pencil between their fingers. Drawing with a computer used to mean fumbling around with a clumsy mouse that jumped off its pad whenever it hit the edge of the virtual paper. The graphics and "undo" features were nice, but it was hard for some artists to switch from paper to a computer.

Gone are the days of having to choose between the two. Today's forensic artists use touch pads and tablets—computer hardware that replaces a mouse with a wireless pen and a writing pad that responds to even the tiniest bit of tilt or pressure. With these tools, drawing and erasing on screen feels just like doing it on paper. There are even different nib styles to create thin or thick lines. Artists can scroll and zoom, shade and color with just a click of their wireless pen.

When the image is done, it can be saved as a digital file, so artists can immediately send the image to police, who then can get a high-resolution sketch of a suspect out to the media as fast as their Internet connection can send it. The technology is great news for impatient detectives and artists with sore wrists. (But bad news for suspects on the lam.)

Time can work against the interview in other ways. A witness may be coming forward to share the details he remembers months or years after the crime happened, for example, and the artist then has to prompt the witness to remember enough details to create an accurate sketch. To get past some of these challenges and to save time, forensic artists bring an important tool with them to an interview—a group of visual aids. These pictures can help witnesses remember and describe individual parts of the offender's face so the artist can draw them accurately.

The *FBI Facial Identification Catalog* is one of the most common aids artists use to help witnesses describe faces in detail. This catalog has pictures of almost any kind of facial feature imaginable, grouped by ethnic types and general shapes. There are pages of eyes, for instance, that are broken down into smaller sections such as "bulging eyes." There are pictures of flat noses, sharp noses, and long noses, full lips and thin lips, and beards and mustaches in many different styles. A witness looks through these various features and picks out those that look most like the individual features of the suspect. An artist can then pull the features together into a face that the public might recognize. This process often moves along far more quickly than if the witness has no visual aids to look at when describing a face.

Even with the help of a facial identification catalog, forensic artists must give witnesses privacy and time to think. Artists can draw only what the witness remembers—no more and no less. They also cannot lead the witness in any way. In other words, they cannot make suggestions that might cause witnesses to doubt what they remember. The artist's job is to suggest nothing about a suspect's appearance, but instead, to let the witness remember, and then illustrate that memory on paper.

Making the Sketch

The actual work of drawing a face from a witness's memory is a complicated process. At the same time, the artist's goal is to keep the drawing simple. Facial features that are especially noticeable—thick lips, bushy eyebrows, high cheekbones, a double

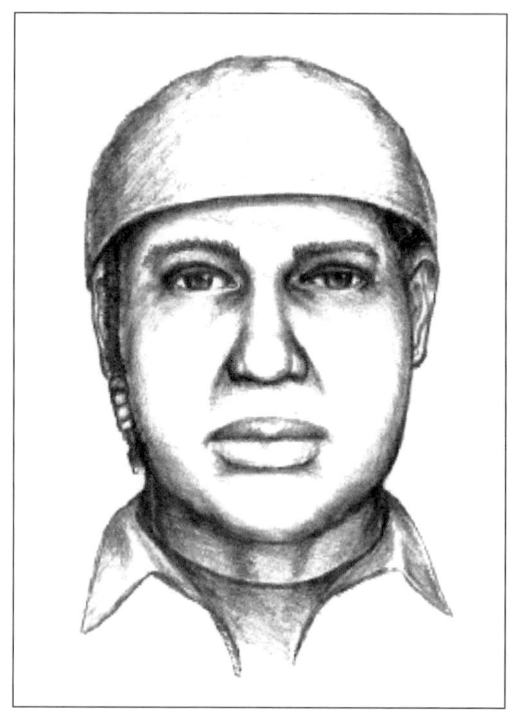

The artist who created this composite sketch of a suspect in a 2008 store shooting in Illinois used subtle shading to illustrate the size and shape of his facial features and included the specific detail of a hair braid, a unique aspect of his look that could help lead to his identification.

chin—are important to include in the sketch, because these are things that might make the face recognizable to people who are seeing the sketch for the first time.

Adding too many details other than the most prominent features, however, is something forensic artists try to avoid. Not only does it take up valuable time, but it can also make a drawing too specific to be useful. "It is far better to have a sketchy, haphazard drawing that brings in the perpetrator of the crime," says Gibson, "than to drive the witness to distraction and burnout by spending too much time making the sketch 'look good.'"[7] Even sketchy drawings, though, must look like actual human faces. This is why the artist must have a strong background in the basic principles of drawing and shading, along with comprehensive training in how to draw the particular elements of human faces. A cartoon-style picture with sharp outlines of facial features may not look enough like a real face to bring any calls in to the police's tip line, and therefore, effective composites use shading, not sharp outlines, for features such as lips, noses, and eyes and the places where the face rises and falls around them.

Drawing a human face, as forensic artists do, is similar to accurately drawing a mountain. The land rises and falls, but drawing these changes in height requires skillful shading, or the image will appear more like a big mound of swirls and circles than like an actual, realistic mountain. Drawing a human face takes training and practice in shading to show depth and slope. Noses in particular are like a little hill on a human face, and they must be shaded instead of outlined in order to look real. This takes a lot of training and practice. Many artists who master the shading of a nose concentrate so much on that aspect that they overlook the nose's size. A common mistake in composite sketches is making the nose too long, which in turn can make the whole face look very different than the person it is supposed to resemble.

Eyes are other trouble spots. Because they are made up of many components—the lids, the lashes, the eyeballs, the irises, the pupils, and the eyebrows—they are very difficult to draw accurately. Misrepresenting the tilt of an eyebrow or drawing lids too high or low can completely change the look of a face. An artist who does not get the details of the eyes right may create a drawing of someone that nobody will recognize. This is, in part, what makes forensic art such a difficult specialty even for someone with excellent drawing skills.

Every forensic sketch needs the main features of the face (eyes, nose, lips, and ears) drawn realistically, but even with these features, the drawing may not look much like the offender. This is especially true if the witness remembers the details inaccurately. Fortunately, says Gibson, "some of the more obvious features, the things that make a person unique, are not always the eyes, nose, or mouth."[8] Sometimes, the details that the witness remembers most clearly are not the position of the cheekbones or the width of the nose, but a tattoo or other unique feature that could result in a positive identification, even in a drawing whose other elements do not resemble the perpetrator exactly.

Hair, Metal, and Ink

One goal of any forensic sketch is to show at least one thing about the suspect that will make someone in the community recognize him. Forensic artists are generally careful not to add too many specific details, because if they get the specifics just a bit wrong, it can completely change the look of the person in the sketch. The result of their efforts, therefore, is often a fairly generic drawing that looks like a lot of people who are that same gender, race, and age. Although sketches like these can still be useful in giving police a general idea of what a suspect may look like, the most useful drawings are those that look like only *one* person. Once the artist has the basic facial features on paper, he or she then asks the witness about certain specific details such as hairstyle, scars, tattoos, or any other features that might transform a generic sketch into a recognizable one.

Hair is one of the most important features of any composite drawing. "The hairline on your suspect is a large feature and a distinct, easily noticeable identifier,"[9] Gibson says. A bald man looks very different from one who wears dreadlocks, for instance, and a woman with straight bangs stands out from one with curly hair. Even identical twins, with different hairstyles, will look unique. For men, facial hair—a mustache or beard—is another valuable feature for a forensic artist. Whether a suspect had a beard or a mustache, and if so, what it looked like, are other things that often stick out in a witness's mind. Such details, even more than eyes or lips, can result in calls and leads from the public. Even if the suspect has changed his hairstyle or shaved off a mustache or a beard, says Gibson, "his acquaintances will still remember his facial hair and notice the change."[10]

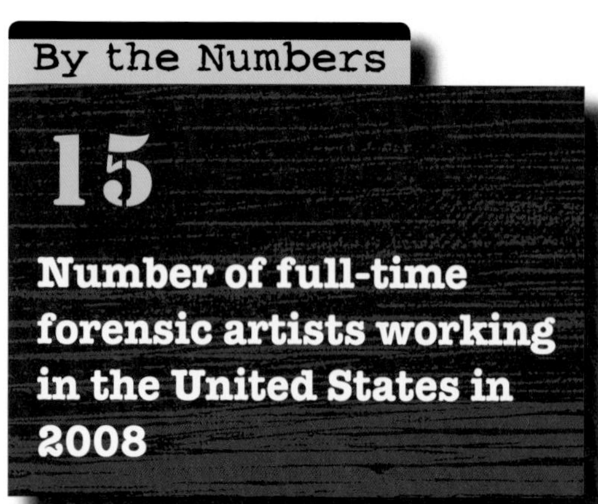

Like hair, other important features of any composite drawing are facial piercings or tattoos. These end up helping forensic artists a great deal. The one

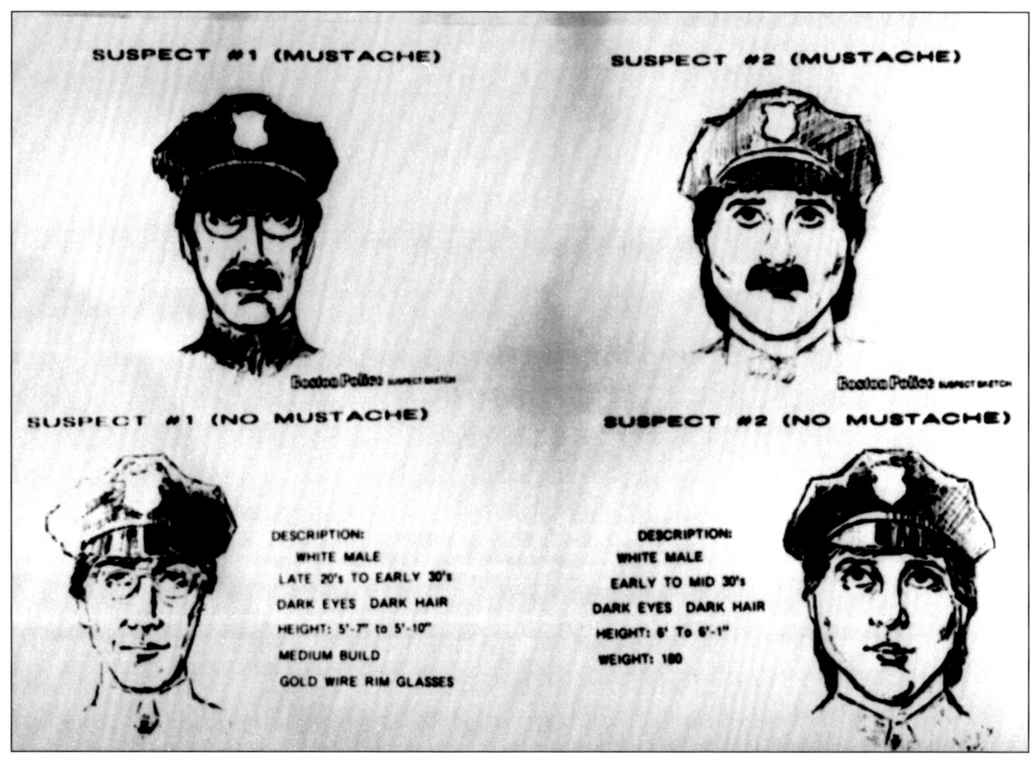

The FBI issued composite sketches of two suspects in a 1990 museum robbery, depicting them both with and without facial hair after determining that the men, who were dressed as police officers when they committed the crime, may have also used fake mustaches as part of their disguise.

thing a witness might remember well about an offender could be a unique tattoo on the person's face or neck, and if the artist focuses on this one detail and draws it well, the rest of the portrait can be completely inaccurate—even the wrong ethnicity or gender, in fact—but still lead police to the offender if a member of the public recognizes the tattoo and tells police the name of the person who has it.

Similarly, scars can be invaluable to a sketch. Acne scars, for example, commonly turn up in forensic sketches, and although they are not easy to draw, they are memorable to witnesses and make an important difference in the look of the finished sketch. Scars from injuries can be more useful still. A crescent-shaped scar on a person's forehead or cheek will stand out, much like a tattoo does, as a memorable feature not only to the witness but also to anyone who knows the suspect. As with tattoos, scars shown in a sketch can be used to track a suspect down even if they are the only details of a sketch that turn out to be right.

Dressing the Perpetrator

Once the facial features of a forensic sketch are drawn, one task remains for the artist: drawing a neck and shoulders. These are important features of a portrait, because without them, the head in the picture seems to hover unnaturally. These details also help to capture extra information about the person, such as body size, that can be hard to show in any other way. Necks can be short and thick or long and skinny, for example, and shoulders can be broad or they can sag. The neck and shoulders also give the artist a chance to draw some of the clothing a witness might remember.

Witnesses often remember a person's clothing even more than a face. They can usually recall whether a man was dressed in a T-shirt or a business suit, for example, or whether a woman had on a red blouse or a white halter. Clothing is a detail many people pay attention to when surrounded by strangers. They may take note of a fashion they like or hate, a logo they recognize, or clothing that stands out because of its color, size, quality, or attractiveness. People are likely to pay closer attention to the kind of clothing a stranger is wearing than to the shape of the person's nose or the color of his eyes, partly because clothing can be observed without appearing to stare at someone. This means witnesses may stand a better chance of remembering details about clothing than about facial features.

Drawing clothing benefits a forensic drawing because it gives the public additional clues about the personality, the age, and possibly even the occupation of the person in the picture. Rarely do forensic sketches show people in clothing as specific as a baseball jersey with a team name and number on it or a waitress uniform with a name tag on the chest pocket, but even the difference between a T-shirt and a dress shirt or a turtleneck versus spaghetti straps can be a hint to the suspect's personality and character. Criminal investigators have learned that men, in particular, tend to dress much the same way every day, so it is likely that a suspect shown wearing a polo shirt in a forensic sketch probably wears a lot of polo shirts. Thus, a

The infamous composite sketch of Theodore Kaczynski, the criminal known as the Unabomber, whose identity was pursued for almost twenty years before his capture in 1996, was dominated not by the suspect's facial features, but by the prominent glasses and hood as described by a witness who encountered Kaczynski in 1987.

clothing style might spark recognition for someone who sees the composite sketch.

Accessories such as hats and glasses help round out a forensic sketch. Many offenders wear these items when committing crimes, perhaps in an effort to disguise themselves, and it is fairly easy for most witnesses to remember the shape, color, and style of a hat or a pair of glasses. Gibson says that a hat in a drawing has the added benefit of helping the artist show how large or small the suspect is. "Since most hats are made about the same size," she explains, "you can indicate really large or rather small suspects by sizing the hat proportional to their head in the drawing."[11]

Manuals such as the *FBI Facial Identification Catalog* can help witnesses quickly narrow down the exact style of hat or glasses they remember. Sometimes, they point out a large hat and wide, dark sunglasses, and the artist may begin to fear that the finished sketch will show a face too disguised to help the case. Even when a forensic artist feels a finished sketch is not likely to be useful to police, she must train herself to leave the sketch alone. "For legal and practical purposes," Gibson says, "you can sketch only what was seen during the crime."[12] As soon as the witness says that a sketch looks like the person he saw, the artist must put her pencil down, hand the drawing over to the police, and go on to the next assignment.

Facial Reconstruction

Forensic artists are also in the business of giving faces to the dead. Learning the identity of a deceased victim is as important to crime investigations as learning the identity of the suspect. Some forensic artists, therefore, specialize in reconstructing what people looked like when they were alive.

Identifying bodies is a common challenge faced by police departments. Whenever human remains are discovered, investigators have a lot of pressing questions. Most importantly, they want to know the victim's name.

According to Karen T. Taylor, one of the leading forensic artists in the United States, it is necessary to give a name to human remains quickly. "You can't easily commence a death investigation," she says, "without first knowing the victim's identity."[13] Not all bodies in need of identification are murder victims. People who die in any kind of accident that caused severe trauma to the body may need to be identified, for example, but whatever the circumstance, police often need an identification in order to determine what happened during the victim's last moments and to decide whether a crime was committed.

Police are also ethically compelled, out of respect for the victim and the victim's loved ones, to make an identification. "Law enforcement agencies are regularly presented with challenging cases of unidentified deceased persons," says Taylor. "It is both their statutory and moral obligation to make every attempt to identify these individuals."[14] Some forensic artists use a mix of artistic talent and scientific knowledge about the structure of the human face to recreate what the person looked like in life.

The Living Dead

The idea that a human skull could be a canvas for a sculpture is not new. Artists and scientists have long been fascinated by the idea of giving long-buried skulls a new face. Archaeologists and historians are interested in uncovering ancient mysteries by identifying Egyptian mummies or in discovering how an ancient Mayan warrior might have looked before weathering thousands of years in the ground. One of the earliest attempts at facial reconstruction was performed in the 1890s by physician Wilhelm His, who asked a sculptor to model a face on the skull of musician Johann Sebastian Bach.

His's concept of sculpting the face of a dead person is basically the same process that takes place in the studios of modern facial reconstruction artists. The process is called three-dimensional facial reconstruction, because the finished

A forensic artist carefully sculpts the details of the facial muscles from clay in an effort to accurately reconstruct a face from the plaster cast of a skull.

product is a touchable, three-dimensional face, usually made of clay right on the victim's skull. The artist's ability to do this task well could be the detective's only hope for identifying the victim. Pathologist Ian Hill says that sometimes the only method of identification at a police department's disposal is the "physical identification by a relative or friend, who is using the person's physical appearance to recognize him or her."[15] Once a relative or friend comes forward claiming to know the victim, police begin making the dental or DNA comparisons they need to scientifically confirm the identity they are seeking. Because this initial claim of identification by loved ones or acquaintances is often what gives police a clue to work from, forensic facial reconstruction can be very valuable for identifying unknown victims.

Puzzle Pieces

In May 2003 a hiker was walking his dog in the ski town of Mammoth Lakes, California, when his pet sniffed out a human skull by the side of the trail. Investigators who were called to the scene soon discovered a shallow grave nearby that contained the rest of the body. Enough of the partially buried corpse remained for police to recognize evidence of a probable stab wound.

"From the first I assumed this was a homicide," says Detective Paul Dostie of the Mammoth Lakes Police Department. "People don't stab themselves then cover themselves up with dirt."[16] Dostie needed to identify the victim, however, before he could start investigating how the body might have ended up in the woods in the first place. To help with this task, he sought out a forensic artist skilled at facial reconstruction.

In the case of the Mammoth Lakes victim, as in every case like it, the forensic artist was part of an important team tackling the mystery from many different angles. A facial reconstruction artist can contribute one piece of the puzzle by artistically reversing the processes of decomposition and creating a picture that a friend or relative of the victim might recognize—a picture that could bring in an important tip or lead in the case. "Forensic art provides the connection between an unidentified deceased person and the records needed to identify that person," says Taylor, describing how a reconstruction is just one step in the crime-solving process. "I have often categorized my role as that of 'middle man.'"[17]

Digging Up Details

Before they begin to put a face together, reconstruction artists need background details about their victim, especially the person's gender and age. The size of the victim is important, too, because the facial features of an overweight victim will look very different than the same features drawn on a person who was slender. To gather clues that can guide the reconstruction, a forensic artist often looks at evidence collected from the crime scene or burial site, such as pieces of the victim's clothing. A tank top and low-rise jeans suggests the victim was young and female while a floral blouse and polyester slacks might suggest an older female. Sometimes clothes still have tags that indicate a person's size. Clothes, jewelry, and other accessories found at the site where the body was discovered might give the artist an idea about the victim's personality, too, such as whether the person wore conservative styles or was a flashy dresser. Personality can be a helpful characteristic for the artist when he or she sits down to re-create a lifelike appearance of the victim.

Forensic artists often work with an anthropologist—a scientist who studies human remains—to deduce from the bones details such as the victim's gender, size, and age. Anthropologists can tell whether a skeleton is male or female, for example, because certain

By the Numbers

25%

Approximate percentage of the unidentified bodies reported to the U.S. National Death Index each year that are determined to be homicide victims

bones are shaped differently depending on gender. The victim's height is easy to figure out by measuring the lengths of bones. A person's age can also be determined—if the bones show signs that they were still growing, the person was a child or teen at the time of death. If bones are frail and brittle, they probably belonged to an elderly person. If there are the marks of pregnancy and childbirth on the bones of the hips and pelvis, the person was a mother.

The artist also looks at the skull and figures out the main facial features of the person whose face she is going to bring back to life. "The artist and anthropologist collaborate to construct the facial features of the unknown individual on the basis of the underlying cranial structure,"[18] Taylor says. Skulls themselves tell stories about the person they belonged to, and an artist must pay attention to these stories before she attempts to put flesh back onto bone.

A Face from the Grave

Police determined that the woman whose remains they found in Mammoth Lakes had been dead six to nine months. Since it was May, her body had spent a cold and snowy winter in its grave. Weather, burial conditions, and animal activity all affect the rate at which a body decomposes, and the skull that police handed over to the forensic artist was in a state of decay—meaning it still contained flesh. For many forensic artists, handling bodily remains such as these, parts that have not quite decomposed, is one of the most disturbing aspects of the job. "I have to be able not just to see the grisly scene set before me, but to look past it," forensic artist Lois Gibson says, describing how she copes with the often gory subject matter of the facial reconstruction process. "I can create something beautiful out of something horrific."[19]

Because the flesh changes so much in death—it shrinks and splits, it bulges and sags, and its color might change—even bodies that are discovered fairly soon after death may bear little likeness to how they appeared in life. "The easily changeable nature of

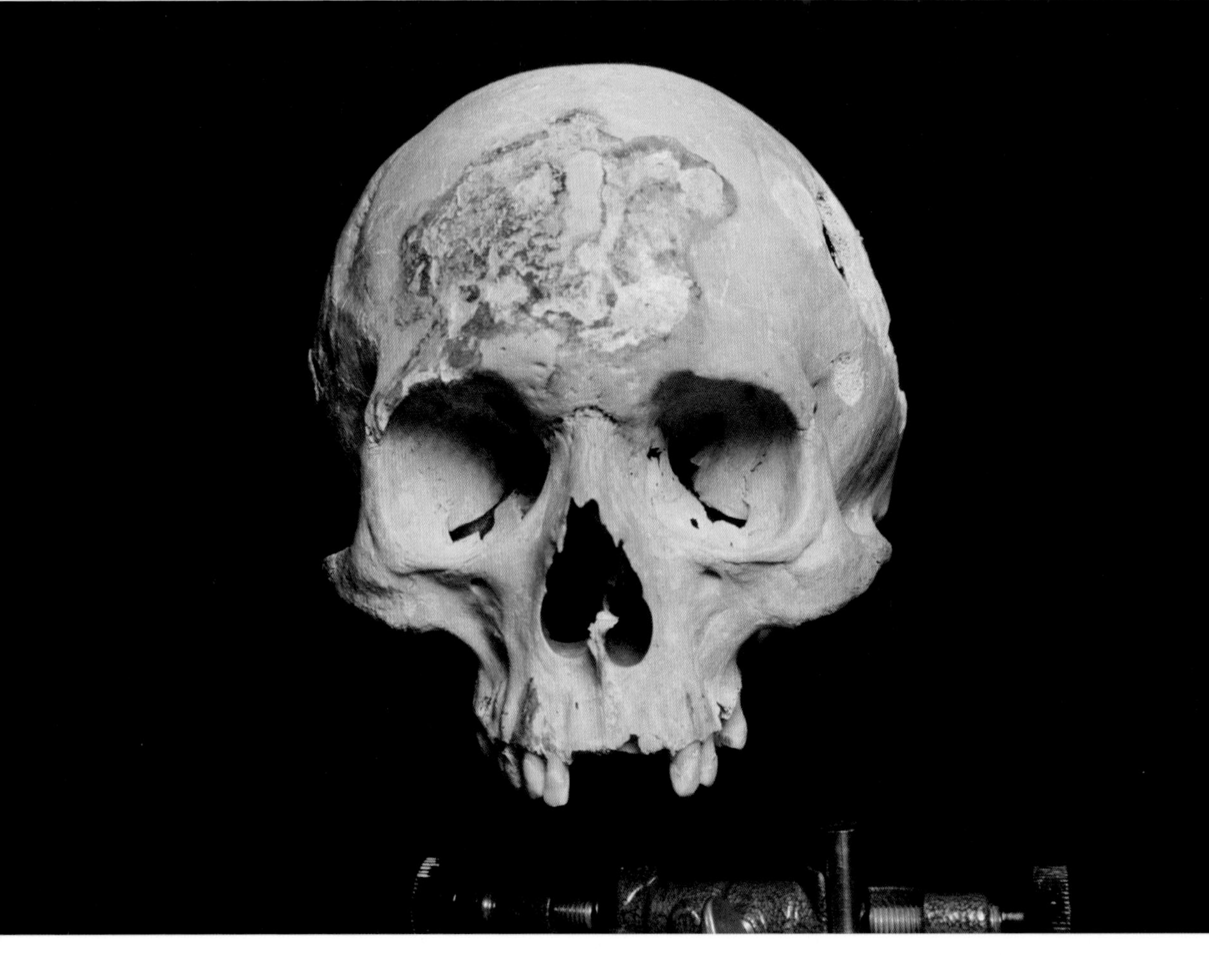

The features of a bare skull provide a forensic artist with the basis for facial reconstruction.

physical appearances presents potent challenges to any attempt to use them as a means of identification," says Hill, "even in ideal circumstances where there has been little or no postmortem degradation."[20] Many reconstruction artists, therefore, prefer to work from scratch. There is rarely enough left of a face to see how the person really looked. Certainly, there will be no twinkle in the eyes, no smile to the lips, none of the lifelike things an artist can give back to the face. Usually, any flesh remaining on the skull is dissolved away in a strong solution of hydrogen peroxide, and the artist is presented with a clean skull to work on.

A trained artist can begin to determine from the shape of the skull the outline of a distinct and unique face. Decisions

A Face-Lift Long Overdue

In 2005 an anthropologist and a medical examiner in New York were asked to create a facial reconstruction based on X-ray images of a human skull. They decided the skull was that of a young man in his late teens, probably from the northern part of Africa.

They were right—the X-ray images were of the 3,300-year-old skull of ancient Egypt's famous boy king, Tutankhamun. A group of curious scientists had wanted to see whether the U.S.-based team would reach the same conclusions as teams in France and Egypt.

The similarities in the scientists' findings showed that facial reconstruction, however old the subject and wherever in the world it is performed, is probably right on the money.

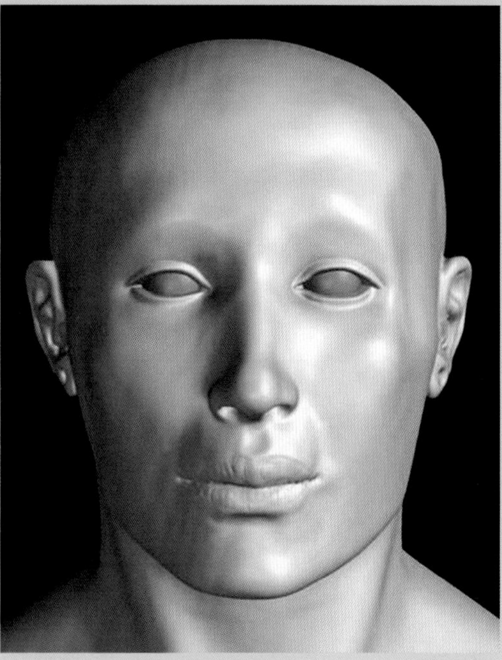

Forensic scientists and artists from the United States, France, and Egypt used modern facial reconstruction techniques to create a computer-generated image of the face of King Tutankhamun, based on the pharaoh's famous remains.

about where to begin adding flesh are not merely artistic. They are made using very specific data—measurements of tissue depth, or the thickness of the facial tissue as it would have been in life all over the face.

Adding It All Up

Knowing the subject's gender, race, and size are crucial to beginning the reconstruction process, because the depth of the tissue at various points on the face tends to be fairly constant for men and for women, depending on their weight and their racial group. The thickness of an African American man's forehead just over his right eye, for example, is likely to be about the same for all African American men of the same weight. It is likely to be different for Asian or Caucasian men, for women, or for men who are overweight.

Scientists who study facial tissue have come up with a group of tissue depth scales, or lists of measurements of the average

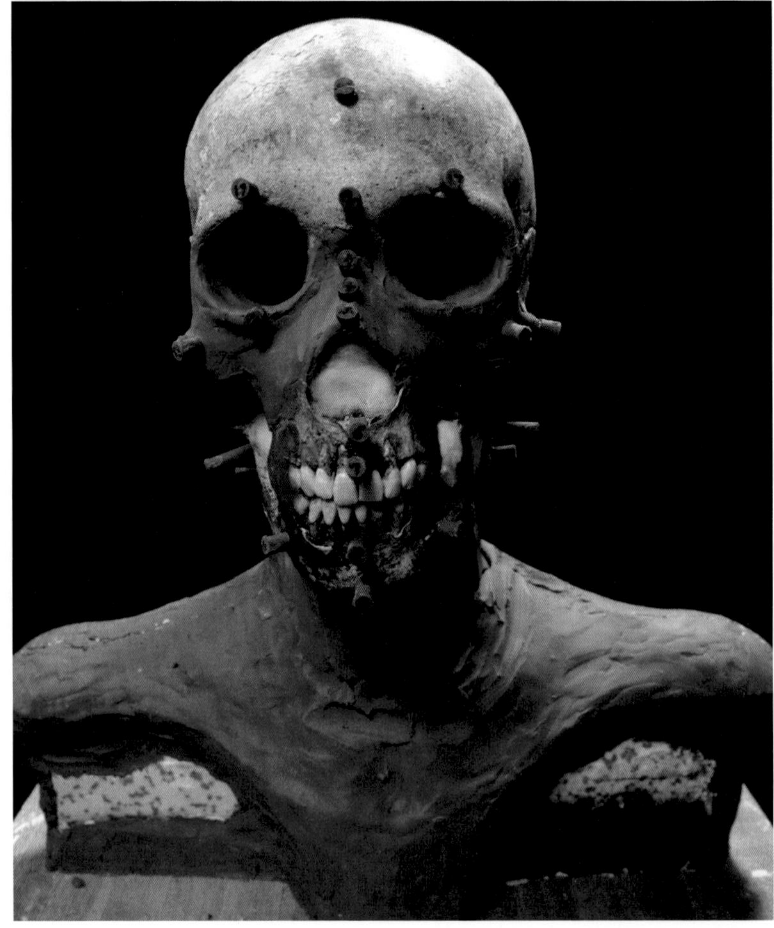

Forensic artists consult a standard list of tissue measurements based on gender, race, and body size in order to properly place a series of rubber markers indicating tissue depth on a skull, a key step in accurately recreating the face's shape and features.

depth of tissue at many specific points on the human skull. There are scales for the faces of men and women of all the major human races and for different body sizes. A forensic artist must choose one of these scales before beginning a facial reconstruction, and the choice is based largely on the research the artist has already done on the victim. When scientific, tissue-depth data are combined with the specific contours of one individual skull, a unique human face will begin to take shape, one that hopefully looks like the person to whom the skull belonged.

By the Numbers

32

Number of tissue-depth markers glued to the skull for a typical facial reconstruction

"The theory behind facial reconstruction is that in the same way that we all have unique faces, we all have unique skulls," says Caroline Wilkinson, a forensic artist with the University of Manchester in England. "It is the small variations in the shape, form and proportions of the skull that lead to the significant variation in our faces."[21] With this special combination of the tissue depths that best fit the victim and the unique lines of the facial bones, a forensic artist can begin to put a face back onto the skull in her hands.

Expressions in Clay

Artists who perform three-dimensional facial reconstruction mold a lifelike face with clay, either directly onto the unidentified victim's skull or onto a precise plastic model of the skull that has been made especially for the facial reconstruction. Using tissue-depth data from the proper scale for the victim's gender, race, and size, the artist cuts a series of rubber markers to the length of these depth measurements. These markers are then attached at the proper places on the skull, and the artist begins to fill in the spaces between them with clay. As the clay is built up to the proper depth at each marker, cheeks, lips, a nose, and a forehead begin to appear on the skull. These clay features start looking much as the skin probably did while the

Creating a Three-Dimensional Facial Reconstruction

Forensic artists who sculpt a face onto a skull, using clay, follow these basic steps:

1. The skull is mounted onto a table using a short pipe or pole to hold it steady.
2. A tissue-marker scale is chosen, based on the gender, race, and weight of the unidentified person, to help the artist choose the right tissue depths for the different parts of the face.
3. Tissue markers are cut, using the tissue-marker scale.
4. The tissue markers are glued onto the proper places on the skull.
5. Artificial eyes are put into the eye sockets.
6. Clay is spread onto the skull, using the tissue markers as guides.
7. The clay is painted to add eyebrows, lip and cheek color, facial hair, and other details.
8. Hair, clothing, and accessories are added to finish the reconstruction.

owner of the skull was alive. The finished product is a life-sized object that can be viewed from all sides.

Once the clay face is complete, the technical part of the job is done, and the artist turns his or her attention to the final touches that make a clay face look human. Eyebrows and eyelashes are added to frame a pair of artificial eyes. A wig is chosen, based on hair evidence from the victim's remains or the artist's best guess about gender, race, and age. Paint is added to bring lifelike color to cheeks and lips. If any personal items were found with the body, such as glasses or a scarf or necktie, these items are added to the sculpture.

As with composite sketches, the forensic artist must know when to call a sculpture complete. It is not a piece of art, but a piece of *forensic* art, headed not to a museum but to investigators and possibly the media. The artist puts in just enough detail to make the face lifelike, and then the process must end.

"By allowing artistic ego to interfere," says Taylor, "the artist risks adding incorrect information that may actually detract from the correct information and *discourage* recognition and identification."[22] Forensic pathologist Martin P. Evison agrees, warning forensic artists against putting too much into their art, specifically, too much of themselves. "There is a well-known tendency," he says, "to incorporate one's own facial features into a reconstruction."[23] Like a composite sketch, a facial reconstruction is better left a little vague. The goal is for someone to see something they recognize in the face, not to recognize every single feature.

Often facial reconstructions, like composite sketches, must be done quickly in cases when a crime has just happened and the crime scene is fresh. In fact, when there is no time to wait for a traditional clay reconstruction, a process that usually takes at least a week, detectives may instead order a two-dimensional facial reproduction—one that is drawn, not sculpted.

A Face in Two Dimensions

With the advances in photography technology that have come about since the days of Wilhelm His, it is sometimes just as accurate to draw a facial reconstruction on a flat piece of paper as to sculpt one onto a skull. Sketching the reconstruction can also be more practical, especially when the skull is too fragile for the sculpting process.

"Extremely fragile skulls may not be strong enough to bear the weight of clay for a sculptural reconstruction," says Vernon J. Geberth, a former lieutenant commander of the New York City Police Department. "In such cases, particularly if the

Facial reconstructions that result in two-dimensional drawings, such as this composite based on the skull of a murder victim found in New Orleans in 2004, can be created by hand by skilled forensic artists or by specialized computer programs.

damage is in the facial area, a two-dimensional approach may be taken."[24]

Whichever method is used, drawing or sculpting, the process of applying tissue depth markers to the skull is the same. "Two-dimensional facial reconstruction follows the same preparatory steps by the artist as those for the three-dimensional method,"[25] says Geberth, but instead of applying clay to fill in the spaces between tissue-depth markers, the two-dimensional artist takes photographs of the skull, a frontal view and a side (profile) view, and does the reconstruction on these. The artist places both photographs of the skull side by side on a drawing table, then covers them with vellum, a transparent paper. Using the shape of the bone and the tissue markers as a map, the artist begins sketching a face back onto the skull. Drawing the reconstruction this way, instead of sculpting it, can save time, money, and the actual skull itself.

Computer Reconstructions

For the same reasons that two-dimensional drawings are sometimes chosen over three-dimensional sculptures, computer-created images may also be chosen. Facial reconstructions are, after all, a mathematical process that requires computing. Betty Pat. Gatliff, an accomplished forensic artist whose many projects include the facial reconstructions of several victims of the 1970s serial killer John Wayne Gacy, says math formulas help artists decide where facial features should go and how large or small they should be drawn.

Gatliff explains how artists use math to decide how wide a nose should be: "We measure across the nasal aperture, which

A crime lab computer shows the process of digital facial reconstruction, which provides a level of speed, accuracy, and flexibility that is impossible to achieve in sculptures or hand drawings.

is the hole where the nose was. That gives us the total width, and we increase it by ten millimeters, which would be five on either side."[26] These measurements fit into another formula for calculating how far the nose should stick out from the face. "We use two measurements," Gatliff says, "the width and projection, and when you connect it to the bridge, that establishes the nose. That's the way I've done it for thirty-five years, and it works."[27]

Other formulas are used to calculate the shape and placement of eyelids, lips, and other features. These details are difficult or impossible to determine from just looking at the skull, but they are very important for successfully creating a lifelike portrait from a skull.

Computers are an ideal tool for precise facial reconstructions. They can perform math calculations instantly, and they also can adapt images with little effort. With the proper software, it is simple to add effects such as weight or age to a face, try out different hairstyles, change eye color, or even give the person a suntan. These are changes that take considerable time to make on a clay or sketch reconstruction. Computers are even able to use medical technology, such as laser scanners and magnetic resonance imaging (MRI), to provide thousands of tissue-depth measurements for a head and face, compared to traditional clay or pencil reconstructions that are made using fewer than three dozen tissue markers.

Evison is a strong believer in the possibilities of computer-generated reconstructions. "Abandoning the traditional landmarks in favor of approximately 10,000 measurements collected from MRI records will represent a significant increase in the precision and accuracy of facial reconstructions," he says. He predicts that in the years to come, computer images will be "accurate, rapid, repeatable, accessible, and flexible."[28]

Just the same, science and technology are only half of the process. The other half is the art of giving human character to an image, and this is something computers cannot do. Evison admits that although computer images do have many

One-Hour Skull

A handheld laser scanner, somewhat similar to the ones store clerks use to reach across the counter and scan big items sitting in your cart, is now being used by some facial reconstruction experts to scan skulls.

When the artist aims the scanner at the skull, a red laser beam moves across the features of the bone and creates the same image, in three dimensions, on a computer screen. The computer program then connects to a special machine that builds an exact copy of the skull out of resin, the material used to make plastic.

The artist goes to lunch, and when he or she returns an hour later, the copy of the skull is ready to be sculpted into a facial reconstruction.

Artists who are squeamish about touching an actual human skull can now sculpt on a plastic copy instead. Investigators who need the skull for other purposes can have it back. Once the victim is identified, family members can sleep better knowing their loved one's remains were not clumped up with clay. And everyone can rest assured that if the head is fumbled and dropped during reconstruction, it is only a plastic copy.

advantages over reconstruction sculptures and sketches, the computer models "presently lack the sophistication and accuracy of life."[29]

A computer may turn out a facial reconstruction that is mathematically perfect, but what the victim's loved ones may be looking for—and the one detail to which they may respond—could be a twinkle in the eye or a slightly amused turn of the mouth. No computer, at present, can give a picture this very human touch. "So much of what is incorporated into the process is artistic instinct based on experience from drawing thousands of faces,"[30] says Taylor. Police depend on this artistic experience to create a face that may strike a chord among people who knew the victim.

A Cold Case Gets Warmer

Gatliff was the artist whose hands brought the Mammoth Lakes murder victim back to life. A week after she received the victim's skull, her three-dimensional sculpture of the woman's face was complete. Photographs of this sculpture were shown on news programs in California and Oaxaca, Mexico, where investigators had determined, from biological and chemical analyses of her remains, that the woman was probably born and raised.

"When the police drawing and reconstruction photograph were shown in Oaxaca, a woman said that the Gatliff facial reconstruction looked like her stepdaughter,"[31] says Dostie. Thanks to Gatliff's expert hands, the Mammoth Lakes Police Department was a big step closer to solving the crime. The woman's killer, however, was still on the loose, and investigators knew that the longer he avoided capture, the harder it would be to find him. After all, suspects age. If many years pass before they are caught, they may become harder and harder to recognize. In cases that drag on for years, forensic artists may be called upon to perform yet another valuable service in an unsolved case: age-progressing a picture.

Age Progression

Just before Thanksgiving in 1971, a middle-aged accountant from Westfield, New Jersey, shot and killed his four children, his wife, and his mother. Then he turned on all the lights in the house, packed a suitcase, and slipped out the front door. Police unsuccessfully searched for this killer, John List, for eighteen years.

Nearly two decades after the killing spree, forensic artist Frank A. Bender created a sculpture of the murderous accountant, instinctively aging his artwork to look like what he thought List might look like in the present day. Bender's three-dimensional reconstruction appeared on television, and it brought in a phone call that finally led police to List. He was living a new life under a new name with a new wife in Colorado, but he looked very much like Bender had predicted he would.

Forensic artists like Bender help police put names to faces. Their talents capture the looks of possible suspects for police to track down and question. They can also return faces to accident and murder victims to give police a place to start with identifying unknown bodies and providing answers in unsolved cases. Even when the police already know exactly who they are looking for, as in the case of John List, an artist's talent can help the case by putting a new face to an old name. These are cases in which artists have a great deal of information to go on from the start, even pictures of the person they need to draw. The challenge is that the pictures are old ones. The artist is asked to age the face in the photographs in the hope of finding a person who has been avoiding police detection for years.

Finding Fugitives

The television show *America's Most Wanted* first aired in 1988. Each week since its first episode, the show has featured criminals whom police across the country are trying to catch. In most of these cases, the mystery is not what the person did or to whom, but where the criminal is now. Forensic artists have a leading role in the success of *America's Most Wanted*, which in the spring of 2008 led to the capture of the show's one-thousandth featured

Forensic artist Frank Bender displays an age-progressed bust of murder suspect John List, who was on the lam for nearly twenty years until Bender's work led to his identification and arrest in 1989.

criminal. Part of the show's success depends on broadcasting forensic artists' depictions of what fugitives, who have been on the run for years, might look like now. The capture of John List was one of the show's earliest success stories.

To provide the kind of updated images featured on *America's Most Wanted*, forensic artists use a process called age progression. They add a few years, or even a few decades, to a face in a picture the police have on file. This makeover modernizes the person's appearance into one that people living with or around the fugitive today might recognize. The long list of fugitives caught after being featured on *America's Most Wanted* is evidence that age progression works.

Turning the Clock Forward

Age progression is different than composite sketching or facial reconstruction because the artist already knows exactly what the person looks like—or at least, what the person used to look like. Adding age-related changes, however, takes much the same skill and knowledge that is needed for drawing composite sketches or reconstructing decomposed faces. The artist must know the structure of the human face well in order to add the right kinds of changes to age a picture. Specifically, the artist needs to know how human faces grow, develop, and change over time, and also how they stay the same. Forensic artist Karen T. Taylor says that "expressions may contribute to a certain 'look' throughout life." This quality, she says, "is what allows us to recognize childhood and adolescent friends as adults when we see them at class reunions."[32]

Looking for a characteristic expression in existing photographs of a fugitive, therefore, is an important starting point for an artist who is doing an age progression. Photographs serve as an outline for the aging features the artist will add to a face. There is more to the process than making existing wrinkles look a little deeper and turning hair gray. The artist must also predict how the shape of the face itself is likely to change over time. Skin sags with age, but in what directions and to what

A forensic artist aged murder suspect Richard B. Thomas twenty-five years in this computer-generated image, which led to Thomas's arrest on charges of killing a Philadelphia police officer in the early 1970s after it was shown on the television program America's Most Wanted *in 1996.*

degree is something the artist must figure out in order to accurately age the face in the photo.

Another step in performing an age progression is looking at photographs of the fugitive's close relatives, such as parents, grandparents, and siblings. The way people age is often inherited. Therefore, a close look at pictures of a brother or sister, a mom or a dad, or even a person's grandparents will give the artist valuable clues about whether to add a double chin or take away half of the person's hair.

An artist also needs a few details about the fugitive's personality and lifestyle before starting an age progression. People's personal habits, diet, and how well or how poorly they take care of themselves have a direct effect on the way their faces age with time. "You have to look at what lifestyle they're into," says Amber Weiss, a forensic artist for the DeKalb Police Department in Illinois. "Are they heavy into drugs? Do they spend a lot of time outside?"[33] Cigarette smokers, habitual sunbathers, and lifelong overeaters may age somewhat differently, for example, than people with healthier habits. A forensic artist often interviews people who knew the fugitive before he or she disappeared to figure out what kind of lifestyle the person had. Physical signs of different health habits can be factored into an age progression.

All of this information can be helpful, but in the end, solid knowledge of how human faces age and change is the best tool an artist has. Artists are often called upon to create age pro-

Age Regression Answers an Old Question

The Ohio Historical Society has a picture of a woman it just cannot identify. Records about the woman's portrait give her name, Mary Worthington Tiffin, the wife of the state's first governor. But Mary Tiffin died in 1808, and the clothing the woman in the photograph is wearing was not in fashion until a decade or two later. The woman in the picture cannot be Mary Tiffin.

The Ohio Historical Society was so bothered by the mystery that it called in a forensic artist to perform an age *regression*, instead of an age progression. Using the same techniques artists use to predict how a person will age, the artist worked backwards to predict how the mystery woman would have looked as a child.

There was a family resemblance, in the age-regressed photo, to pictures of other Worthington children. The woman in the picture may have been a family member of the real Mary Worthington Tiffin, a relative who lived long enough to enjoy the ladies' fashions she was wearing in the picture. As for her real name, the historical society may never know.

gressions for subjects whose lifestyle and habits are not known and for missing children whose lifestyle and habits are still developing.

The National Center for Missing and Exploited Children (NCMEC) generated an age-progressed photo, center, of what kidnapping victim Johnny Tello might look like at age seven, based on an actual photo taken when the boy was a toddler, left. The photo on the right shows Johnny after he was found.

Toddler to Teen to Twentysomething

In June 1996 a four-year-old girl and her two-year-old sister were kidnapped from their father's home in Houston, Texas. He did not see them again for eleven years. When the girls were finally found living with their mother in Costa Rica, it was because of an age-progressed photo posted in a Wal-Mart store. One of the girl's classmates saw the picture and recognized it immediately. The sisters were finally reunited with their father because of a portrait drawn from a few childhood pictures that were more than a decade old.

This case is just one of many success stories of the National Center for Missing and Exploited Children (NCMEC), an organization whose age progressions have been used to help find more than 120,000 lost or kidnapped kids. Like *America's*

Family Abduction

Johnny Tello

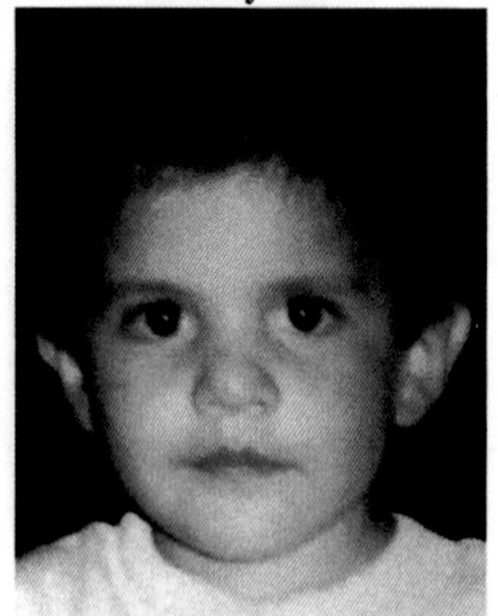

Birth: 08/31/1990 Race: White/Hisp
Missing: 10/04/1993 Ht: 3'00" Wt: 35 lbs
Eyes: Brown Hair: Lt. Brown Sex: Male
Missing From: Dallas, TX
Age Now 11 Yrs United States

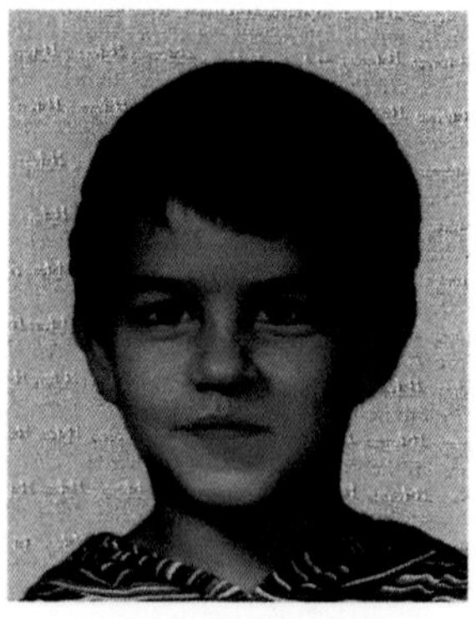

Age Progression by NCMEC

On: 02/03/1998

Recovery Photo

On: 08/31/1999

Johnny's photo is shown aged to 7 years. He was abducted by his non-custodial father.

Face Surgery for the Future

The same scientific principles that help forensic investigators predict what children will look like as teenagers or adults is also helping plastic surgeons. Children born with birth defects, such as cleft palate (a split in the bone that makes up the roof of the mouth), often need surgery to repair the places where the bones of their face are not growing normally.

Replacing bones of the face or adding to them can change the way a child will look as he grows. Plastic surgeons want to give the child a face that will grow with him, one that will still look natural when he is an adult. These surgeons often use the same kinds of age-progression techniques that police departments use to predict how a lost child will naturally change as he or she ages.

Surgeons must predict the growth lines of the child's bones and leave enough room for the growth that will take place in the head and face.

Just like forensic age progressions, surgical age progressions are very personal, and they depend on accurate calculations. No two people age exactly the same way, so no two age progressions (or surgeries) can be exactly alike.

Most Wanted, the NCMEC gets pictures out to the public in the hope that someone will recognize the children and call police. The difference between the NCMEC and *America's Most Wanted* is that the NCMEC is trying to find missing children, not criminals, perhaps making the quest to find them even more desperate. "In cases of missing and abducted children, the need for an 'up-to-date' look of the child is critical,"[34] says Taylor.

It can be far trickier, however, for forensic artists to add years to faces of children than to faces of adults. For one thing,

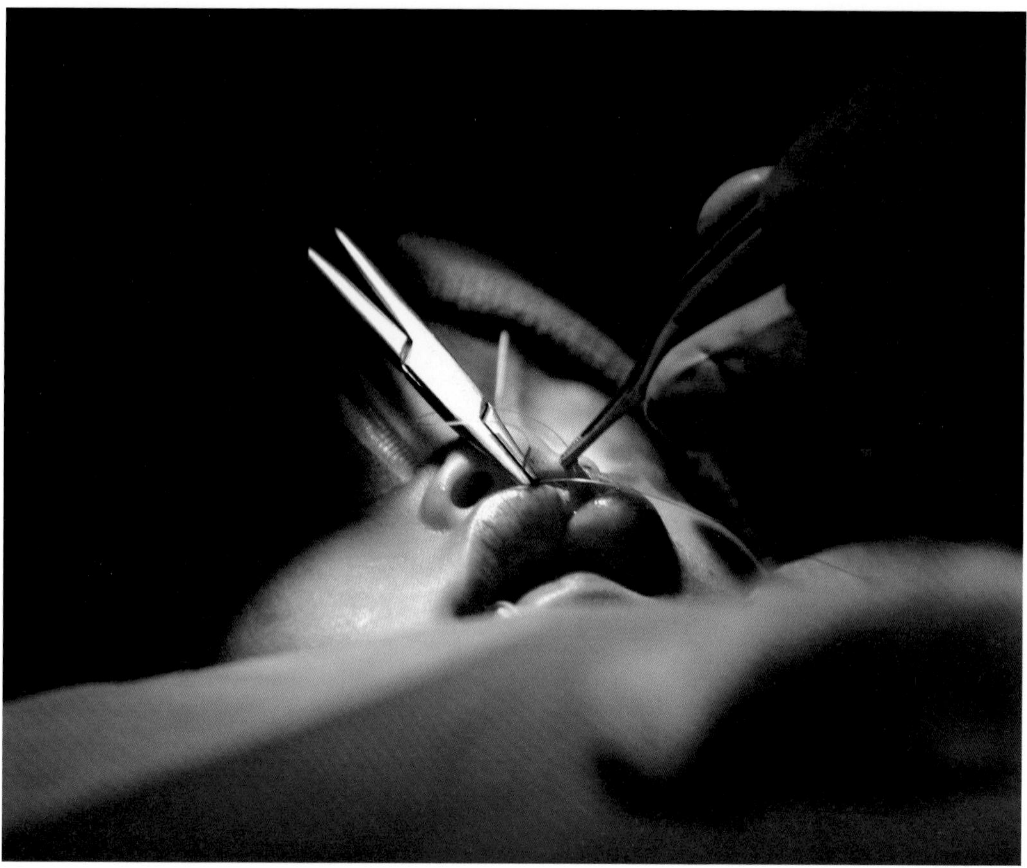

Surgeons repair a toddler's cleft palate. Such procedures are often done with the assistance of age-progression technology so that doctors can ensure that the reconstruction allows for the child's face to retain a natural look as it grows.

an adult's skull has already taken on the general shape it will hold throughout life, and age progression of adults is therefore focused mostly on changes to skin and hair. Very little about a young child's face, however, will look the same after ten years have passed. The skull itself goes through tremendous changes as its bones grow and develop. The teeth fall out and new ones grow in. Skin gets thicker and may grow facial hair or develop pimples. Hair changes color. And next to nothing may be known about a child's lifestyle, diet, or sun exposure when he or she has been missing a long time. "The image of a child who's been missing for years is the more challenging task," says author and forensic psychology professor Katherine Ramsland. "The artist has to rely on a number of factors to get it right."[35]

Creating successful age progressions that solve cases keep forensic artists motivated in spite of the challenges. An artist who not only understands what kinds of changes a face will need but who can also combine this knowledge with artistic talent possesses a winning combination of skills for creating the kinds of recognizable images that brought the kidnapped Texas girls home.

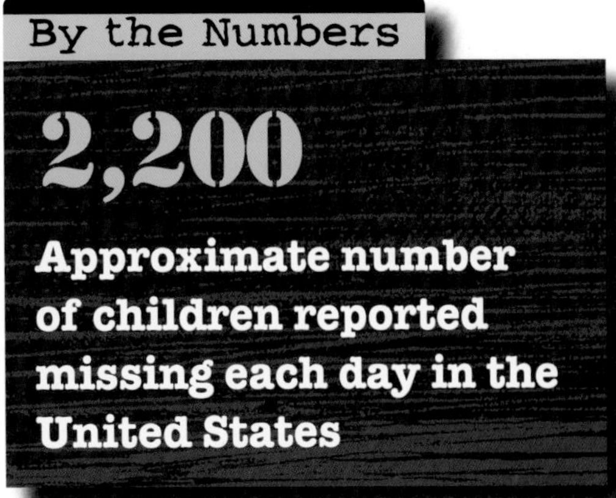

Where to Begin

A lot of research goes into every successful age progression before the artist even sits down at the drawing board. A face, Taylor says, "should be carefully studied and compared with any available family photographs. There may actually be a resemblance of specific features to grandparents or other relatives that is stronger than resemblance to parents."[36] Particularly useful are photos of family members taken when these people were the same age as that to which the victim's face needs to be progressed. "All of this involves training,"[37] says Taylor.

The age-progression process itself begins by finding specific places called reference points on the face in the photograph. These points are used to draw triangles over the parts of the face that change over time. After the reference-point triangles have been drawn, the artist can experiment with the sides of certain triangles, lengthening or shortening them to determine which facial features need to grow and change, and in what proportions.

In children, for instance, the face gets wider and longer with age. The chin grows down and out. Eyes get narrower. The mouth grows wider and the bridge of the nose rises. The top half of the head also gets bigger. Changing the shapes of the various triangles laid over the picture is a quick way to determine how to make these important changes to the proportions of the face. How many or how few of these changes are made depends on what the artist knows about human biology, what she sees in family photos, and the target age she is aiming for. "Knowing the age of the child when the picture was taken," says image analysis expert John C. Russ, "and using data that describe the relative rates of growth of different parts of the head and face . . . a picture can be adjusted to compensate for these changes and show the way the child's face would be expected to appear at a different age."[38]

Like all forensic art, deciding on a new face shape for an age progression requires a special mix of science and logic, artistic skill, and usually a bit of the artist's gut feeling. In the end, the outline of the face the artist has created will hopefully be a close match to the shape of the person's face now, a face that someone watching television or walking out of a department store might look up and suddenly recognize.

Fine Detail

Few people are able to escape showing certain signs of age. Gravity tugs at the corners of the mouth and the lids of the eyes. Faces also get used to the expressions their owners make throughout life—expressions that usually stay the same from childhood into old age. Frowners frown, grinners grin, and over the years, the lines from these expressions get carved into the skin. Changes—those that gravity makes to every face and those that are specific to one face alone—are what make it possible for forensic artists to add years to photos in ways that are recognizable, often strikingly so.

Forensic artists depend on their knowledge of how faces and facial muscles work and move to get an age progression right. All faces eventually wrinkle, but it is not enough to merely add wrinkles to an age-progressed face at random. They have to be the right wrinkles, in the *right* places, because very specific wrinkles and creases form after years of making a certain smile or frown or raising one eyebrow a certain way. The eyes, especially, are places where wrinkles must be accurate in an age-progressed image. "There is usually a strong retention

Knowledge about how specific facial features develop and age over time is key to the creation of age-progressed images, such as this composite of Charles Arlin Henderson at age twenty-seven, right, created by the National Center for Missing and Exploited Children in 2007, sixteen years after the boy disappeared at age eleven.

of a 'look' in the eye area as we grow," says Taylor. "Childhood expressions may last a lifetime."[39] A few crows' feet in the right places can help bring a child's photo into the second or third decade of life.

More than Just Wrinkles

Forensic artists add other important changes to faces, too, depending on the age they are trying to target in their age progression. A chin that the artist believes would have drooped with time needs shadows beneath it. Cheeks may need shading to look less plump and more hollow. In elderly persons, there might be circles under the eyes, and eyebrows and eyelashes may have grown thin. Teenagers may get acne. Young men often have a hint of hair on their upper lip and along the jawline.

Teeth, too, take a lot of an artist's time during an age progression. Teeth are one of the most important parts of any face. For a teenager, teeth may need to be drawn both with and without braces to provide examples of very different possible

> **By the Numbers**
>
> **1.5**
>
> **Number of times a child's skull doubles in size between birth and the age of two years**

looks. If the artist is working from a photo of a six-year-old who is missing both front teeth, the age-progressed photo will be created with permanent front teeth in place. For an elderly person, teeth might have grown yellow, and a few might be missing. Whatever changes an artist makes, the teeth are one area of the finished face that must be right. "Lack of attention to the teeth can produce a very incorrect or even distorted look in a finished updated image,"[40] says Taylor. This is perhaps the last structural change the artist will make to the face before giving the age progression its final touch: clothing and accessories.

The Fashion Makeover

As with any composite sketch or facial reconstruction, hair and clothing can make the difference between the success and failure of an age-progressed image. After all, a fugitive whose last good picture was taken in 1979 when he had long hair and a mustache will almost certainly have updated his look in the years since. A picture of a little boy in blue overalls, likewise, will require a much different outfit if anyone is to recognize a picture of him as a teen.

Adding or taking away a beard or mustache, cutting or coloring hair, putting makeup and jewelry on women and teens, and using accessories such as glasses and hats are crucial decisions in a successful forensic age progression. Providing several possible variations of a person's look, based on different hairstyles, clothing, and accessories, is particularly important in the age progression of fugitives, people who generally do not wish to be found and may go to great lengths to make themselves look entirely different than they did in their "former" life. These people may change their look often, so the more different appearances and styles the artist can give to the drawing of the fugitive, the better the odds that someone will recognize one of the pictures.

In cases of kidnapped children, too, the success of an age progression may improve if the artist provides a few different possible versions. Although kids or teens who have been abducted may not realize that police and family are looking for them and may not be deliberately masking their appearance, predicting their "look" is challenging nevertheless. The most recent available photos of a missing child may have been taken when she was very young, long before she had a chance to develop her own sense of style. It is the artist's job to guess how a teenager whom no one has seen in years would decide to wear her clothes and hair. As much as possible, artists try to make these determinations based on what they know about the individual from interviewing family members and friends.

The Technology Behind the Face

The need to generate multiple images quickly, especially showing the same basic face with multiple hairstyles, accessories, and types of clothing, has led to the use of computers. With a computer program, Taylor says, "it's a simple matter to provide multiple alternate looks without having to draw the whole thing over again. It's more efficient to do this with a computer."[41]

However, computers cannot do the work alone. It is not true that computers can create accurate age progressions with little dependence on an artist's time and skill. This false belief underestimates how difficult it is for an artist to predict the specific ways one person's face will change over time. The facial reconstruction of John List, for example, did not involve a computer at all, just Frank A. Bender's instinct about the kind of man List was and how that would predict the kind of *older* man he would turn out to be. Although a valuable tool, a computer is no match for the skill and instinct of the artist who operates it. Computers cannot replace the training in art, psychology, and biology that forensic artists use to do their job.

Today's computer-generated images do, however, reflect an ever-advancing digital world that benefits the different fields of forensic art. In fact, the same technology that can speed up the process of age progression is revolutionizing the forensic use of photographic images of all kinds. If a photograph exists in a criminal case, no matter how poor its quality may be, modern technology can often make it useful for the forensic investigation.

Image Enhancement

In the early morning hours of March 5, 2008, twenty-two-year-old Eve Marie Carson, student body president of the University of North Carolina, was shot to death 1 mile (1.6km) from the university campus. According to investigators, the gunman probably did not even know the name of the pretty young woman he gunned down. He then stole her sport-utility vehicle and her bank card and sped to an automatic teller machine (ATM) and withdrew cash. ATMs have security cameras, though, and police quickly retrieved a black-and-white photo of the man who used her bank card. He was clearly wearing a Houston Astros baseball cap, and police believed they now knew the face of the man who had killed Carson. But the surveillance footage held more information than police first realized.

Forensic Image Experts

For decades, cameras have operated almost like undercover members of a worldwide police force. Surveillance and security cameras keep a watchful eye on banks, parking lots, and stores, and fast-thinking witnesses often have the chance to use personal cameras to record crimes in progress. The assassination of President John F. Kennedy on November 22, 1963, was captured on film by a sightseeing cameraman and became one of the most famous examples of videotaped crime footage in history.

A photograph has been the turning point in many police investigations, because cameras are honest. Unlike eyewitnesses, they do not have emotional slips of memory or recall the wrong details. The person *taking* the picture, on

Baltimore police use a network of security cameras to monitor activities on the city streets. Footage of crimes captured by security cameras can provide helpful—but sometimes imperfect—information to investigators.

the other hand, might not be making an honest record of events, and the person who tries to make sense of the picture might be mistaken when deciding what the photo shows. Investigators often need the help of forensic image experts, people who can professionally assess a picture to decide how honestly a photograph represents the crime. "The camera never

Enhancing a Photograph

Forensic image experts are often asked to help investigators clear up a poor-quality photograph so they can see details better. Using a computer, forensic image experts generally follow these steps:

1. The image is scanned into the computer and uploaded into a photo editing software program. The program is set to keep track of all changes to the image.
2. The image is enlarged to a size that makes it easier to see.
3. Any lighting problems in the photograph are fixed. This may involve lightening areas that are in shadow or darkening areas that show too much glare.
4. Necessary changes to color are made by adding color to a black-and-white image or using color filters to block out certain background colors that make parts of the image hard to see.
5. The number of pixels per square inch is increased if the photo is blurry or if there are lines or pieces of writing that need to be seen more clearly.
6. The image is then separated into layers. Certain layers that need to be seen by themselves are pulled out of the image and placed against a clear background.
7. A permanent record of the changes made to the image is created, which includes what the changes showed that was not visible in the original image.

lies," says Geoffrey Oxlee of the Kalagate Imagery Bureau in England. "It merely records what it sees, but this is only useful if the imagery recorded is properly and correctly interpreted."[42]

Becoming a Forensic Image Expert

Job Description:
A forensic image expert works in a law enforcement laboratory or as a freelance contractor to develop, process, and enhance photographs used in investigations. The forensic image expert may be asked to process photos from crime scenes and autopsies and may also enhance images in various ways to make them more useful for investigations. The forensic image expert is responsible for keeping detailed records of images and what has been done to them.

Education:
Forensic image experts usually need a minimum of one semester of college-level coursework in photography and digital imaging.

Qualifications:
Most positions require two years of photography-related work experience in the field of forensics. Some police departments provide on-the-job training.

Additional Information:
Forensic image experts must have strong knowledge of photography equipment and software and must be organized. The ability to learn new software is essential because technology in this field changes rapidly. Public speaking skills are also important, as they may be asked to testify in court.

Salary:
$10,000 to $50,000 per year

Photo evidence has become more common with the prevalence of security cameras and camera cell phones, but rarely is this footage high quality. Surveillance camera photos are often fuzzy and many times fail to capture the one angle that shows the suspects' faces. Witnesses may be running while taking pictures, producing blurry, shaky photos, often of people's backs instead of their faces. And since many crimes happen at night, photos may simply be too dark to be of much value. Still, there are ways to make even poor photo evidence potentially useful. Forensic image experts are the people who specialize in making bad photos look better.

Photo Magic

The photograph of the man using Eve Carson's bank card made him the lead suspect in her murder. The ATM image also showed that he was driving what appeared to be an SUV the same color as Carson's missing Toyota Highlander. An important clue would have been overlooked, however, if investigators had not taken the ATM footage to a forensic image expert. The enhanced image showed something police had not noticed before—there was a passenger in the vehicle's back seat. The original black-and-white image had not provided enough contrast to reveal him, but the enhanced image added color to the picture that brought the passenger into view. Without the forensic image expert's help, police might never have known there were two people possibly involved in the crime.

According to Herbert L. Blitzer and Jack Jacobia, who manage the Institute for Forensic Imaging in Indianapolis, Indiana, simple changes to a photograph can be the key to solving a crime. "Small details within an image that might not appear important when first encountered may later be discovered to be crucial to the investigation," they say. "By capturing details in a photograph they are not only preserved, but their characteristics may also be examined more carefully and in a way that permits them to be placed within the context of a broader investigation."[43]

Image enhancement has a long history, and most often, experts at enhancing images use their skills to fix or improve bad photographs for private citizens. Image experts rescue overexposed wedding photos, preserve antique portraits of ancestors, and airbrush the faces of cover models for magazines. However, police departments, too, sometimes seek out the

Investigators in North Carolina used image enhancement techniques to study an ATM security camera photo taken of a man using the bank card and driving the car of murder victim Eve Carson in order to identify suspects in the March 2008 crime.

services of these experts when they need help brightening, sharpening, angling, or magnifying a snapshot that could be important evidence of a crime. In the digital age, there is little that an experienced image expert cannot do to an image.

Investigators analyzed surveillance video that captured the image of a man believed to have information about a double murder at a Kansas bakery in 2002, then provided the public with a photo of a shirt like the one he wears in the video in hopes that someone might recognize him.

Revealing the Invisible

The last day of 2006 was the last day of George Azarian's life. The disabled sixty-one-year-old was crossing a street in Revere, Massachusetts, when he was struck and killed by a car, and the driver sped away without stopping. No one came forward to say they had seen the crime. "Investigators had little to go on," says Megan Woolhouse, a reporter for the *Boston Globe*, "except for some grainy video from a security camera."[44]

The security camera was on the roof of a nearby building, and it was the only witness to the hit-and-run. The camera's

> **By the Numbers**
>
> **2,000**
>
> **Number of surveillance cameras added to Beijing's Olympic Stadium for the 2008 summer Olympics**

footage showed that a light-colored, sedan-style car hit Azarian and then drove away, but this was not enough to help police track down the right vehicle and culprit. They took the footage to a film enhancement expert who was able to sharpen the image. Although the car's license plate number was still too blurry to read, the make and model of the vehicle became clear: It was a silver Dodge Intrepid. Police officers pulled records of all the owners of Dodge Intrepids in the area and eventually tracked down the one that killed Azarian.

The photo enhancement that solved this case was nothing fancy—the expert simply sharpened a poor-quality image from a standard surveillance camera. It was, however, enough to solve a case that might otherwise have gone cold. Most examples of image enhancement are just this simple. Forensic image experts do as little as possible to photos or footage, because they know they may be holding the single clue available in a case as well as an important piece of evidence that could be used in a court of law.

Thou Shall Not Tamper

"The morality of retouching becomes tenuous when dealing with real events," says Gwen Lute, author of *Photo Retouching with Adobe Photoshop*. Image experts, she explains, must be careful not to misuse their knowledge and tamper with photo evidence. "A retoucher must be careful not to be drawn into illegal activity, such as manipulating a picture for a court case or an insurance settlement."[45]

An important rule for forensic image experts is to keep their adjustments as simple as they can. In fact, they often use the very same processes and programs available to amateur photographers using any home computer. "The truth is, most

They Have Their Eyes on You

From the moment anyone walks through a casino's door in Las Vegas, Nevada, a man upstairs is watching. So are all the casino surveillance teams in town. Thousands of cameras record faces in every major gambling place in the city. A surveillance team sits in a special room watching dozens of television screens, all looking for suspicious activity, such as signs of cheating on the game floor.

Surveillance is big business in Las Vegas. Casinos invest in the best technology available. They even have facial recognition software to quickly compare the face of one suspected cheater to the casino's database of photos of known cheaters. Casinos also link their photograph databases, so a cheater at one place will be just as quickly recognized when he moves across the street to another place.

The gambling industry is the champion in this kind of technology. Even the military and the FBI turn to casinos for new ways to track bad guys.

Casino security personnel use a variety of sophisticated surveillance techniques, including facial recognition software, to track suspicious activity and identify cheaters.

By the Numbers

500 DPI

Minimum resolution, in dots per inch (dpi), of scanners used by the FBI (a typical fax has a resolution of 200 dpi)

of the time it is not necessary to do any fancy adjustments,"[46] say Blitzer and Jacobia. Most images just need slight clarification, and in forensics, the more basic the adjustments made to a picture, the better. Just because a computer can make certain changes to a photo does not mean the forensic image expert *should*. If the photo is later questioned in court, the forensic image expert will need to prove not only what was done to a photo but also how and why.

For this reason, forensic image experts often use familiar computer software, like Adobe Photoshop, to do their work. "It is a program that is widely accepted throughout the imaging world and has already been tested in a few court cases,"[47] say Blitzer and Jacobia. "This does not mean that what you do to an image in Adobe Photoshop won't be questioned." There is a fine line, they explain, "between enhancement and manipulation of an image."[48]

Forensic image experts must keep careful records of all the changes they make to a picture, in case they are asked to prove that they did not tamper with its content. Because they must also be able to tell the court why they made the changes, forensic image experts use software that allows them to track these changes. This provides a valuable record of the steps taken in enhancing a photo. With the change-tracking feature turned on, the forensic image expert can get to work.

Adjusting the Size

Before doing anything to an image, the forensic image expert must upload it into a software program. If the image is digital, this may be as simple as inserting a memory card or a disk into the computer. If it is a two-dimensional image, it must first

NASA on the Case

The same technology NASA (National Aeronautics and Space Administration) has used for years to study storm patterns on satellite video also helps put criminals behind bars. A program called VISAR—which stands for Video Image Stabilization and Registration—helps level out shaky video, clarify blurred pictures of moving objects, and sharpen up still images. In the hands of police departments, this technology means that troubles with nighttime photographs, jittery camcorder footage, and foggy surveillance camera stills are quickly fading into crime-fighting history.

VISAR technology is showing up in many situations. Footage recorded by cameras mounted on police cruisers can be sharpened to reveal license plate numbers and other helpful details. Footage of crimes, recorded by witnesses, can show details that would have been missed before VISAR. Even the military uses VISAR to clear up reconnaissance footage recorded from tanks or helicopters during military operations.

More surveillance cameras are in use than ever before, and cell-phone cameras mean that almost anyone could catch a snapshot of a crime in progress. Paired with NASA's foolproof ways to touch them up, these pictures could mean fewer criminals will get away with their crimes.

be scanned to convert it into a digital file format. Either way, one of the first things done to enhance an image is to change its size.

In digital photography, size has two meanings: the actual dimensions of the photo (its length and width) and the size of the digital file that contains the image. Both kinds of size are important. The photo itself may need to be made larger so that investigators can see details too small to have been seen in the original version—for example, a label on a suspect's clothing or a bumper sticker on a car. Any time a photo gets larger, however, so must the file size. That is, the number of pixels in the image must also be increased. Pixels are the tiny bits, or dots, that make up any picture. An image with few pixels will not have much detail, because the dots that make up the picture are so spread out that the image is fuzzy. A picture with many pixels, packed closely together, is sharper, more colorful, and a better image overall.

A good way to think of pixels is to imagine a shoebox filled with marbles. If you shake the shoebox, the marbles will not move much. But if you were to stretch the shoebox and make it twice as big, the same number of marbles would move around a lot. You would need more marbles to fill the bigger box. Digital photographs work much the same way. Stretching the picture will spread out the pixels, making the image blurry. Adding more pixels to the bigger image is the only way to keep a larger picture as sharp as the smaller original. Therefore, image enhancement experts always pay close attention not only

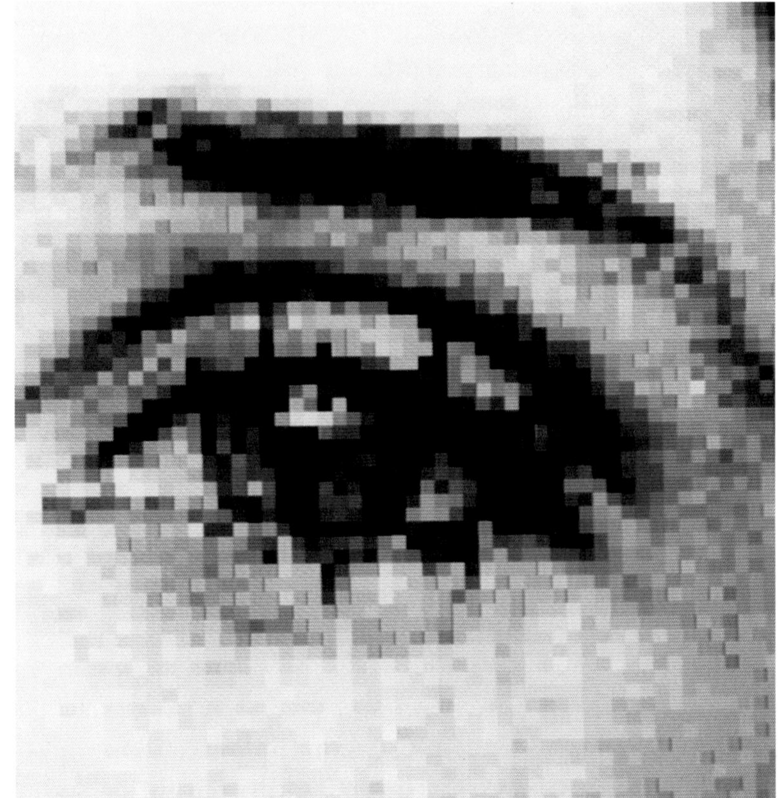

An image of a woman's eye is represented in pixels, the tiny dots that make up a digital photograph that become more visible as the image is enlarged.

to the size of the image but also to the number of pixels per square inch that it contains.

Blitzer and Jacobia say that keeping the same ratio of pixels to image size (the same number of pixels per square inch of the photo) is important to a forensic investigation. When the number of pixels per square inch does not change, they explain, "we have not changed any information in the image."[49]

Perfecting the Picture

Once an image has been sized, the forensic image expert uses a range of tools in the software program to do different things to the picture, depending on what investigators need to see. There are tools to brighten a dim photo or to darken one that is too bright, and these are helpful if an object is in shadow, for example, or if a face is reflected in a window but glare from the sun makes it too hard to see. There are also tools to sharpen the edges of different objects in a photograph, such as blurry shots of license plates or street signs.

Forensic image experts can even break a photograph into different layers—what is in the foreground and the background of the image—and pull out just one layer or piece of an image that investigators want to see. "One of the great additions for us in forensics is the enhanced layer control," say Blitzer and Jacobia. "New layer design features allow you to apply editable gradients, patterns, and solid colors, as well as color adjustments, to other layers."[50] Forensic image experts often take advantage of layering to see things such as fingerprints. The ability to pull forward and darken the fingerprint layer while lightening the background layer can make an otherwise useless fingerprint visible enough to help solve a case.

Paper evidence, such as bank checks and handwritten notes, is a common item forensic image experts are asked help to make clear. Joe Nickell, in his book *Detecting Forgery: Forensic Investigation of Documents*, says investigators often turn to forensic image experts for help studying everything from charred bank bonds to letters written on colored paper. "One use is to enhance writing," he says, and describes an example of a green registration form with writing too faint to be readable. He says a forensic image expert could use a green color filter to subtract the background color. "The form would thus appear white rather than gray," he says, "and the writing would consequently be more legible."[51]

For many criminal cases, forensic image experts work this kind of magic on a poor-quality photo and point investigators to a suspect. It is likely, however, that a forensic image expert's work will be questioned in court. "Because crime scene images are frequently critical to a case, they are frequently challenged,"[52] says Edward M. Robinson in his book *Crime Scene Photography*. Digitally enhanced images are closely studied by lawyers and juries. After all, computer software programs can realistically replace one face with another in a family reunion photo, so the same technology could be applied to wrongly accuse a suspect. Marilyn T. Miller of Virginia Commonwealth University says that "disadvantages in using digital image technology center on issues of court admissibility because of easy image manipulation."[53] Therefore, before any suspect is identified from a photograph, investigators turn to one more kind of expert, someone who can testify in court as to whether the person in the photograph and the suspect himself are one and the same.

The Imagery Analyst

No two people look exactly alike. Even identical twins have enough differences between their faces that their families and close friends can usually tell them apart. On camera, however, it is much harder to tell one face from another—not just for identical twins but for pictures of any two people who look alike.

Courts and juries must decide whether someone is guilty or innocent. They prefer fingerprints and DNA, forms of identification that point to only one person on Earth. Fingerprints and DNA are considered solid evidence in trials because they remove doubt from a case. This is not true of photographs of people's faces. Proving that two photographs show the face of one and only one person is very hard to do. A few shadows in a photograph comparison can easily cast a shadow of doubt on the whole case.

To convince a jury that two photos show the same person, it takes an imagery analyst, an expert in scientifically comparing the images in photographs to decide whether they are the same. This is never an easy task, especially since the only photos investigators have of a suspect may be of terrible quality. Still, cameras do not lie. "A professional cameraman using a combination of unusual angles or harsh lighting could record a photograph of a man in such a way that his next of kin would fail to recognize him," says Oxlee. "Nonetheless, the photograph is still a true image of that man."[54] It is up to the imagery analyst to prove this in court.

Scrutinizing an Image

Imagery analysts know a great deal about photography, physics, and chemistry, as well as computers, digital systems, light spectrums, and geometry. They also specialize in the biology of human faces, culture, and expressions. They use all of this knowledge when deciding whether two photos are of the same face. To hold up in court, a positive identification must come from a qualified expert who supports his claims with as many scientific facts as possible.

"Few people like to be wrong," says Oxlee. "Their minds have a tendency to look for features on the imagery to prove that they were correct and to discount cues that suggest otherwise. In other words, they make the facts fit the case."[55] Oxlee says he does the opposite when he analyzes imagery. Instead of finding similarities, he looks closely for ways that two pictures are *different*. "It takes only one clear difference to enable the analyst to conclude that the persons are not the same," he says. "However, several clear similarities do not prove that they are the same, as many others may share these similarities."[56]

Instead of trying to prove that two pictures are of the same person, imagery analysts try to prove that two pictures are of two different people. They do this with various methods of facial mapping, or the comparison of faces from photographed images. One technique of facial mapping uses computer graphics programs to make both images the exact same size, then rotate them so they are at the same angle (such as head-on or profile). Then one image can be placed on top of the other to see how closely they line up. This method is called superimposing. Another method is to take measurements of different points on both faces and compare them. Common measurements are the distance between the eyes and the width of the mouth from corner to corner. Many points like these are measured on both faces, then compared. If even one major difference is discovered, the faces are not the same.

A third mapping method is to place the images side by side and then top to bottom. Straight lines are drawn between "landmarks" of both faces, such as the centers of the eyes, the tip of the nose, the corners of the mouth, and the tops and bottoms of the ears. These lines make it easy to see if the eyes, chin, and ears of one photo line up with the same features of the other. If they do not, they cannot be the same face. Analysts use these and other techniques to try to prove that two pictures are not of the same person. With this kind of measurable, scientific proof, the imagery analyst can rule out a suspect.

Similar, or the Same?

If an imagery analyst cannot show the images to be different using any method, he will tell police that no differences were found. This is not the same, however, as making a positive identification, which Oxlee says "is only achieved if there is a unique identification mark," or if the similarities "are sufficiently numerous to be overwhelming."[57] Unless both faces have a scar, mole, birthmark, or other unique feature that can be measured and compared precisely, most analysts can only say that two images show no measurable differences—not that they are, without a doubt, the same person.

Still, photographs and footage are often the most convincing pieces of evidence in a case. "Imagery is the only permanent record of what actually happened during an event," says Oxlee. "Therefore, it is very important that imagery evidence, where possible, is made available to the court."[58] Court is where a lot of forensic art ultimately ends up, not just photographs and surveillance footage, but composite sketches, facial reconstructions, and age progressions. When art does make its way to court, it has to be strong enough evidence to stand up to a lot of scrutiny by lawyers, judges, and the jury members themselves.

Forensic Art in Court

Witnesses have been interviewed. Evidence has been collected. Crime scenes have been studied, and a suspect has been tracked down, arrested, and brought to trial. This is the progress investigators and their team of forensic experts like to see with every case. The courtroom, however, brings its own set of challenges to a case. The suspect, now called a defendant during the trial, does not always confess to the crime. Indeed, the defendant is not always guilty and is presumed innocent until proven guilty. The prosecutor is the lawyer trying to prove that the defendant is guilty, and the defense attorney is the lawyer trying to prove the defendant innocent. Both lawyers present all the evidence they have and give their best arguments.

The people who decide whether the defendant is innocent or guilty are the members of the jury—the group of everyday people chosen to hear both sides of the case. Jury members are typical people, who may know little or nothing about the methods used to solve crimes. It is up to the lawyers to present methods and evidence in a way that jurors will understand.

The strongest evidence in the world is of no use if a jury cannot understand it. Lawyers often face the tough job of explaining very technical things to jury members who have never heard the information before, but the best lawyers make the most of this opportunity and try to capture the jury's interest in their side of the case. "What may be routine to the technical expert can be fascinating to a lay juror who is trying to follow the story,"[59] say authors Fred Chris Smith and Rebecca Gurley Bace in *A Guide to Forensic Testimony*. Helping jurors do that—follow the story—sometimes requires an artist's touch.

A Case of Misplaced Identity

Shortly before 1 A.M. on March 9, 1997, rap singer Biggie Smalls was leaving a party in a GMC Suburban when a Chevy Impala pulled up alongside his car. The driver fired several shots into Biggie Smalls' chest. Biggie died moments later.

Two of Biggie's companions saw the shooter and helped police make sketches of the man. One sketch was made the next day. One was made eighteen days later. The two sketches looked nothing alike.

This composite sketch of a suspect in the 1997 murder of rapper Biggie Smalls was created eighteen days after the crime, but not released to the public for another two and a half years.

Suspiciously, neither sketch was released to the media until two and a half years after the shooting. Even then, only the second sketch was released. Police claimed no one had kept a copy of the first sketch made the day after the murder—which is very unusual, because a composite sketch is considered an important clue in solving a crime, and because police departments often carefully store these early sketches.

The "loss" of an important composite sketch was just one of a long string of police mistakes that cast doubt on the whole investigation. Some people believe there were police officers involved in the rap star's murder. The case is still unsolved.

Forensic art often enters the courtroom in the form of visual aids—tools that the lawyers on both sides use to illustrate important evidence in a way the jury will understand.

Crime Scene Sketches

Defense lawyer Leslie Abramson refers to a diagram of the murder scene during the 1995 retrial of brothers Lyle and Erik Menendez, who were accused of killing their parents. Forensic artists create such diagrams in order to help juries visualize details of a crime.

The scene of a crime is often at the center of courtroom battles. The place where the crime happened is filled with evidence and the answers to many questions. How did the perpetrator enter and get away? Where were the witnesses? Where was the victim? Jurors want and need to know the story of the crime, and they usually need to see the place where it happened.

Crime scene sketches are a standard part of crime investigation. Wherever a crime takes place—on a busy sidewalk, for example, or in a bank, or in someone's living room—eventually, police must take down the yellow crime scene tape and allow the area to be cleaned up and used again. Before they do, they must have a record, in photographs and sketches, of how the scene looked right after the crime. The criminal may

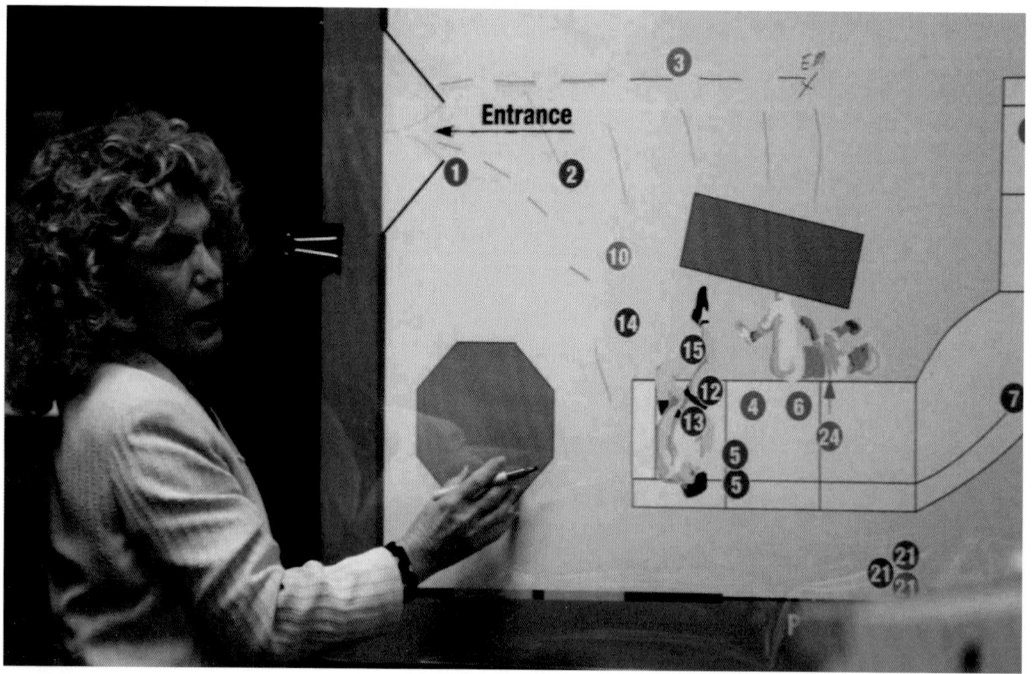

not be caught for months or years, and there will be no way to remember the crime scene exactly unless there are pictures and drawings. "Sketches help investigators recall details of the crime scene," says Barry A.J. Fisher, director of the crime laboratory for the Los Angeles County Sheriff's Department in California. "They also aid prosecutors, courts, and juries to better understand the crime scene."[60]

A crime scene sketch is different than the photographs that are taken at the scene. The photographer is recording specific items that might be important in the investigation and in court: for example, the position and condition of the victim's body, a weapon that may have been used in the crime, or footprints that appeared at the scene. Sketches, on the other hand, show how the entire crime scene looked. "Sketches clarify the appearance of the crime scene and make it easier to comprehend," says Fisher. "Photographs alone are not sufficient."[61]

Sketches usually show a floor-plan view of the crime, as if looking at the scene from straight above. Although they are not meant to be artistic, they are important pieces of forensic art when they are used in the courtroom, showing the position of the victim relative to other objects in the scene as well as the placement of weapons, the precise distance between furniture, doors, and windows, or other details that help to explain how the crime occurred and the condition of the scene when it was discovered. "A crime scene sketch is not considered an architectural drawing," says Fisher. "Sketches sometimes leave out important information or contain errors. Yet despite these drawbacks to and problems in making crime scene sketches, they do provide important information and, when done properly, are very helpful."[62]

Show and Tell

The use of visual aids such as crime scene sketches and photos can be a turning point in a court case. The difference between just explaining to a jury what happened and illustrating it with visual aids can be the difference between a verdict of guilty or

A table-sized model of a subway car and station, created by a forensic artist, is used to illustrate the details of the crime in the 1996 trial of Edward Leary, who was convicted of two 1994 subway firebombings in New York City.

not guilty. "The story is only the beginning," say Smith and Bace. "Showing is as important as telling."[63]

The skills of forensic artists and computer graphics experts may be used to create the kinds of visual aids lawyers depend on in court. Diagrams and sketches of the crime scene may be combined with flow charts showing the events that happened. Graphics and drawings can help explain complicated things such as DNA analysis. Drawings of the bodies of murder victims show exactly how many wounds there were, and where. Computer presentations and slide shows make testimony more interesting and meaningful, and forensic artists can help prepare all of these things.

"Visual aids are being used more frequently in the courtroom," says Janet Vogelsang, a South Carolina social worker who frequently testifies in court. "People are more likely to remember what they see than what they hear. Studies show that jurors will remember 65 percent of a demonstrative presentation after 17 hours, but only 10 percent of oral testimony alone."[64]

Forensic artists usually have training in the anatomy of the human body, and this, along with their drawing skills and knowledge of computer technology, make them a perfect source for medical examiners and prosecutors to turn to when they need to make their case in pictures. In this way, forensic artists may work behind the scenes for a court case. Sometimes, though, they themselves must make a presentation to the jury to explain a composite sketch, an age progression, or other evidence created with their own hands.

Testifying in Court

When forensic artists are called to the witness stand, it is usually as an expert witness because of their special knowledge about art and forensic science. "Since forensic art is one of the most unusual professions," says forensic artist Lois Gibson, "any experience or training will be highly specialized."[65]

As expert witnesses, artists can usually give their opinions about a sketch or other form of art to help prove a case. Sometimes, artists are called to the stand by the prosecution. Sometimes, they are called by the defense. Either way, they may be asked to explain and defend their own art to the jury, usually because it led police to the suspect who is on trial. "The purpose of forensic art is to aid in the identification, apprehension, and conviction of criminal offenders," says forensic artist Karen T. Taylor. "A logical 'follow-up' to production of the artwork is that appearance by the artist in a court of law may be required."[66]

Forensic artists are often asked in court exactly how they came up with the drawing and how certain they are that it is accurate. These can be hard questions to answer, especially if the drawing looks very little like the defendant sitting in front of the courtroom. Gibson, who has testified in more than sixty trials, says, "No artist can do a perfect portrait of a person even if he or she can see that person. Therefore, any jury will accept

A 1979 mug shot of serial killer Coral Eugene Watts is displayed during court proceedings alongside an artist's composite sketch of the suspect in the murder for which Watts was on trial in 2005. The artist testified during the trial that the facial features captured in the sketch, which was based on a witness's description, were similar to those of Watts in the actual photo.

that a forensic sketch will have imperfections. If the artist can explain that certain imperfections commonly occur, it will allow the court to understand the witness was remembering just as well as hundreds of other witnesses to crimes where the proven perpetrator was identified, tried, and convicted."[67]

Just the same, jurors may question the work of a forensic artist. Making a forensic composite requires the witness's memories (which may not be all that reliable) and the artist's ability to put them down on paper (which the jury might also believe is not that reliable). To avoid these problems in court, professional forensic artists are careful to record, or document, what they are doing during every piece of art that they produce. This way, they can easily answer questions that could be asked later in court. They write down the details of their interviews with witnesses, for example. If they are ever asked about their process in court, they can then show their written record of what the witness said and how this information was used to create the drawing. "After all," says Taylor, "the finished drawing is, in fact, the witness' statement and the documentation of his or her memory."[68]

By the Numbers

10,000

The number of innocent people who would be convicted of a crime in the United States each year if the justice system were incorrect just 0.5% of the time

Experienced artists do not ask for specific numbers in their interviews with witnesses, because these are the kinds of details that could later be questioned in court. Artists usually do not ask witnesses for a suspect's weight in pounds or age in years, for example, but instead use terms such as *overweight* or *thin*, *teens* or *early twenties*. In court, specific numbers only set up a case for reasonable doubt that the defendant is the person the witness remembers. If a witness claims a suspect was thirty-five to forty years old, for example, and the artist writes this age on the composite, the defense attorney might challenge the entire sketch if the defendant is only thirty-four. "I avoid exact numerical ages in writing," says Gibson. "If you are not certain about something, do not put it in writing."[69] She says that she actually commits to very little in writing. "No defense attorney has been able to call into question his client's guilt over anything I put in writing on my drawings in court,"[70] she explains.

Whether a sketch looks like the defendant or not, and whether it was well documented or not, forensic art is one area of any court case that is highly likely to be questioned by attorneys and by the jury. Many successful forensic artists never get called to testify during the course of their careers, not because their work is poor quality or because they are not honest and ethical but because forensic art—a sketch or an enhanced photo, an age progression or a reconstruction—is very hard for attorneys to present as reliable proof in court. Although it has helped solve many cases, it has also been known to seal the fate of the wrong person entirely, and this has given it a bad reputation in the courtroom.

Using Sketches in Court

In 1981 Jerry Miller was sent to prison for committing rape in a parking garage in Chicago, Illinois. He spent twenty-five years behind bars for the crime—a crime he did not commit. Miller was freed from prison in 2007, when DNA evidence finally proved he was not the rapist.

Miller's conviction had centered on a composite sketch and the memories of two different witnesses who pointed their fingers at Miller. Sadly, he is not alone in having been both mistakenly accused and convicted. Other wrongly accused people have spent time in jail simply because someone said they looked like the person who committed a crime.

"Mistaken eyewitness identification is a major problem," says attorney Lisa Steele, a member of the National Association of Criminal Defense Lawyers. "Eighty-five percent of the convictions overturned by DNA evidence have involved a mistaken eyewitness."[71]

Some composite sketches are so accurate, and look so much like the defendant, it seems the entire case could be made on the strength of the composite alone. The New York Court of Appeals says this might be the entire problem, if police all along were searching for someone who looked like the composite sketch instead of someone who actually committed a crime: "One thing is certain: if the sketch is right it will resemble the person accused, and if the sketch is wrong it will resemble the person accused. Indeed, the accused—innocent or guilty—is *supposed* to look like the sketch."[72]

This is not to say that forensic artists, even in cases that end in sending the wrong person to prison, have done anything wrong. They are merely putting down on paper what a witness claims to remember about the way the

By the Numbers

12 YEARS

Average amount of prison time a wrongfully accused person serves before being proved innocent

offender looked. In many ways, it is no different than a police officer's taking a witness's statement about what happened during a crime, and courts do not allow witness statements to be used as evidence unless the witnesses themselves take the stand. Because forensic artists do not actually observe the crime or the criminal, some courts consider sketches to

What Makes Evidence Admissible?

Admissible evidence is evidence that juries are allowed to see during a trial. Inadmissible evidence is evidence that is not allowed to be presented in the courtroom.

Evidence may be determined to be inadmissible by a judge for the following reasons:

1. It is unreliable. It does not come from a recognized expert in his or her field.

2. It is hearsay. It comes from a secondhand witness—someone who does not have personal knowledge of the evidence, but who just heard about it from someone else.

3. It would upset the jury too much. Graphic photographs of murder scenes and victims are often inadmissible.

4. It was gathered using illegal methods.

When composite sketches are not allowed in a courtroom, it is usually because they are considered hearsay. The person drawing the sketch did not actually see the suspect or witness the crime.

When enhanced images, such as photographs or video footage, are not allowed in a courtroom, it is often because the process of enhancing them could be considered an illegal method of getting evidence.

Forensic artists and forensic image experts must always be careful to follow legal procedures exactly, or their art may not be used in court.

be hearsay—something one person heard another person say about the crime. These courts do not permit "he said" or "she said" testimony, so forensic sketches cannot be used as trial evidence.

It is important to remember, however, that in any court case a lawyer's argument against the accuracy of a sketch has nothing to do with the artist's ability to interview and draw or with the artist's honesty and integrity. A defense lawyer is doing his or her job by questioning any evidence presented against the defendant, particularly if the only evidence is the forensic art.

Using Photos in Court

Somewhat different problems can turn up when photographs instead of sketches are presented in court as evidence. Unlike a composite sketch, which even the artist admits may not look like the real offender at all, a photograph may be considered a real and true image of whatever is depicted. A long-held belief has been that if a photo exists, then so did the person, object, or scene that the photo shows. In today's world of digital photography, however, this assumption is no longer true.

If it is possible for photographers such as Anne Geddes to show a newborn baby sleeping in the middle of a giant tulip, it is also possible for any photographer or forensic image expert to place an innocent person in the middle of a crime scene. This possibility can cast a hint of doubt on any court case. Therefore, whenever a photograph is used in court, especially if it is one that has been enhanced to make it clearer and easier to see, it tends to breed doubt in the minds of lawyers and jurors.

Just the same, photographs are extremely useful in court. To address concerns that photographs might have been tampered with, forensic photographers use something called a chain of custody. This is a written list of everywhere film and footage have been, everyone who has handled them, and everything that was done to them between the time they were taken or obtained and the courtroom. "All evidence needs to have a chain of custody established," says author Edward M. Robinson, so that the court can be "assured that the photograph being offered in court as evidence actually is an image from the incident in question."[73]

Skilled forensic photographers write down what they take pictures of, when and where the pictures are taken, and what the pictures show. "Counsel may, during cross-examination, question the crime scene investigator about objects shown in photographs," says John Horswell in the book *The Practice of Crime Scene Investigation*. "If there are no notes on the items, it may prove embarrassing."[74]

Even worse than embarrassing, it can raise questions about whether the photograph might have been retouched to make someone look guilty. For example, if a frame of surveillance camera footage has been enhanced, the jury may doubt that the license plate number it shows is real, and wonder if the forensic image expert added in his or her own numbers. Such questions lead some courts to refuse enhanced photographs as evidence in a case, much the way composite sketches may be rejected.

"The knowledge produced by surveillance cameras always involves interpretation," says Aaron Doyle in his book *Arresting Images: Crime and Policing in Front of the Television Camera*. "Those who have the power to interpret the images—who produce the authorized definition of the situation—are the ones who hold the upper hand."[75] Judges and juries may therefore be skeptical of any enhanced image offered as evidence in a case.

Imperfect Proof

Forensic art can be successful even when it is not perfect, and it can do its job even if it can never be used as evidence in a court of law. "Police composite sketches are critical investigative tools," states the New York Court of Appeals. "They winnow the class of suspects from the infinite down to a lesser number of people." However, the court says, "a witness is not a camera

Photographer Brian McCrone displays photos he took of murder suspect O.J. Simpson in 1993 in which the broadcaster and former football star is wearing shoes similar to those that left footprints at the scene of the 1994 murders of Nicole Brown Simpson and Ronald Goldman. Simpson's lawyers at his civil trial in 1997 maintained that the photos had been altered, but lawyers for the plaintiffs presented evidence that they were indeed valid.

and a sketch artist is not a photographer."[76] In other words, no good case can revolve completely around a piece of forensic art, because art is not proof that someone is guilty. Instead, forensic art is a means to an end. "Law enforcement should use this as a starting point, not the end point," says Taylor. "Direct evidence will be needed to secure a conviction."[77]

Forensic artists and forensic image experts are often the ones who give police that starting point. Whether they create sketches or facial reconstructions, enhance photos or perform age progressions, they are part of a larger team of forensic experts who depend on them. For this reason, they have a place of honor on investigative teams working criminal and missing person cases.

Notes

Chapter 1: Composite Sketches

1. Quoted in Matthew Cella, "Sketch of Suspect Heats Up Search for Serial Arsonist," *Washington Times*, February 20, 2004.
2. Lois Gibson, *Forensic Art Essentials: A Manual for Law Enforcement Artists*. San Diego, CA: Academic Press, 2008, p. 1.
3. Gibson, *Forensic Art Essentials*, p. 1.
4. Gibson, *Forensic Art Essentials*, p. 2, emphasis in the original.
5. Ian Hill, "Physical Appearance," in *Forensic Human Identification: An Introduction*, eds. Tim Thompson and Sue Black. Boca Raton, FL: CRC Press, 2006, p. 93.
6. Gibson, *Forensic Art Essentials*, p. 3.
7. Gibson, *Forensic Art Essentials*, p. 28.
8. Gibson, *Forensic Art Essentials*, p. 44.
9. Gibson, *Forensic Art Essentials*, p. 47.
10. Gibson, *Forensic Art Essentials*, p. 55.
11. Gibson, *Forensic Art Essentials*, p. 55.
12. Gibson, *Forensic Art Essentials*, p. 55.

Chapter 2: Facial Reconstruction

13. Quoted in Katherine Ramsland, "The Reconstruction of a Face," truTV Crime Library, www.trutv.com/library/crime/criminal_mind/forensics/art/5.html (accessed May 24, 2008).
14. Karen T. Taylor, *Forensic Art and Illustration*. Boca Raton, FL: CRC Press, 2001, p. 370.
15. Hill, "Physical Appearance," p. 96.
16. Paul Dostie, "Case Number 03-0929: Murder in Mammoth Lakes," *Forensic Magazine*, June/July 2007, www.forensicmag.com/articles.asp?pid=150 (accessed May 9, 2008).
17. Taylor, *Forensic Art and Illustration*, p. 370.
18. Taylor, *Forensic Art and Illustration*, p. 370.
19. Lois Gibson and Deanie Francis Mills, *Faces of Evil*. New York: Kensington, 2007, p. 19.
20. Hill, "Physical Appearance," p. 89.
21. Caroline Wilkinson, *Forensic Facial Reconstruction*. Cambridge, England: Cambridge University Press, 2004, p. 1.
22. Taylor, *Forensic Art and Illustration*, p. 379, emphasis in the original.
23. Martin P. Evison, "Modeling Age, Obesity, and Ethnicity in a Computerized 3-D Facial Reconstruction," *Forensic Science Communications*, April 2001, www.fbi.gov/hq/lab/fsc/backissu/april2001/evison.htm.

24. Vernon J. Geberth, *Practical Homicide Investigation: Tactics, Procedures, and Forensic Techniques*, 4th ed. Boca Raton, FL: CRC Press, 2006, p. 296.

25. Geberth, *Practical Homicide Investigation*, p. 296.

26. Quoted in Ramsland, "The Reconstruction of a Face."

27. Quoted in Ramsland, "The Reconstruction of a Face."

28. Evison, "Modeling Age, Obesity, and Ethnicity in a Computerized 3-D Facial Reconstruction."

29. Evison, "Modeling Age, Obesity, and Ethnicity in a Computerized 3-D Facial Reconstruction."

30. Quoted in Ramsland, "The Reconstruction of a Face."

31. Dostie, "Case Number 03-0929."

Chapter 3: Age Progression

32. Karen T. Taylor, "Forensic Art in Cold Cases," in *Cold Case Homicides: Practical Investigative Techniques*, ed. Richard H. Walton. Boca Raton, FL: CRC Press, 2006, p. 510.

33. Quoted in Dana Herra, "Reyes Sketches Leads for Cops," *Daily Chronicle* (Dekalb County, Illinois), July 15, 2007.

34. Taylor, "Forensic Art in Cold Cases," p. 506.

35. Ramsland, "The Reconstruction of a Face."

36. Taylor, "Forensic Art in Cold Cases," p. 507.

37. Quoted in Ramsland, "The Reconstruction of a Face."

38. John C. Russ, *Forensic Uses of Digital Imaging*. Boca Raton, FL: CRC Press, 2001, p. 74.

39. Taylor, "Forensic Art in Cold Cases," p. 507.

40. Taylor, "Forensic Art in Cold Cases," p. 510.

41. Quoted in Ramsland, "The Reconstruction of a Face."

Chapter 4: Image Enhancement

42. Geoffrey Oxlee, "Facial Recognition and Imagery Analysis," in *Forensic Human Identification: An Introduction*, eds. Tim Thompson and Sue Black. Boca Raton, FL: CRC Press, 2007, p. 258.

43. Herbert L. Blitzer and Jack Jacobia, *Forensic Digital Imaging and Photography*. San Diego, CA: Academic Press, 2002, p. vii.

44. Megan Woolhouse, "Trooper's Work Leads to Arrest in Hit-and-Run," *Boston Globe*, January 26, 2008.

45. Gwen Lute, *Photo Retouching with Adobe Photoshop*. Buffalo, NY: Amherst Media, 2002, p. 7.

46. Blitzer and Jacobia, *Forensic Digital Imaging and Photography*, p. 97.

47. Blitzer and Jacobia, *Forensic Digital Imaging and Photography*, p. 81.

48. Blitzer and Jacobia, *Forensic Digital Imaging and Photography*, p. 81.

49. Blitzer and Jacobia, *Forensic Digital Imaging and Photography*, pp. 100.

50. Blitzer and Jacobia, *Forensic Digital Imaging and Photography*, p. 81.

51. Joe Nickell, *Detecting Forgery: Forensic Investigation of Documents*. Lexington: University Press of Kentucky, 1996, p. 175.

52. Edward M. Robinson, *Crime Scene Photography*. San Diego, CA: Academic Press, 2007, p. 322.

53. Marilyn T. Miller, "Crime Scene Investigation," in *Forensic Science: An Introduction to Scientific and Investigative Techniques*, 2nd ed., eds. Stuart H. James and Jon J. Nordby. Boca Raton, FL: CRC Press, 2005, p. 177.

54. Oxlee, "Facial Recognition and Imagery Analysis," p. 258.

55. Oxlee, "Facial Recognition and Imagery Analysis," p. 258.

56. Oxlee, "Facial Recognition and Imagery Analysis," p. 261.

57. Oxlee, "Facial Recognition and Imagery Analysis," p. 258.

58. Oxlee, "Facial Recognition and Imagery Analysis," p. 258.

Chapter 5: Forensic Art in Court

59. Fred Chris Smith and Rebecca Gurley Bace, *A Guide to Forensic Testimony: The Art and Practice of Presenting Testimony as an Expert Witness*. Boston, MA: Pearson Education, 2003, p. 82.

60. Barry A.J. Fisher, *Techniques of Crime Scene Investigation*, 7th ed. Boca Raton, FL: CRC Press, 2003, pp. 86–87.

61. Fisher, *Techniques of Crime Scene Investigation*, p. 86.

62. Fisher, *Techniques of Crime Scene Investigation*, pp. 86–87.

63. Smith and Bace, *A Guide to Forensic Testimony*, p. 72.

64. Janet Vogelsang, *The Witness Stand: A Guide for Clinical Social Workers in the Courtroom*. Binghamton, NY: Haworth, 2001, p. 83.

65. Gibson, *Forensic Art Essentials*, p. 403.

66. Taylor, *Forensic Art and Illustration*, p. 543.

67. Gibson, *Forensic Art Essentials*, p. 403.

68. Taylor, *Forensic Art and Illustration*, p. 546.

69. Gibson, *Forensic Art Essentials*, p. 397.

70. Gibson, *Forensic Art Essentials*, p. 397.

71. Lisa Steele, "Trying Identification Cases: An Outline for Raising Eyewitness ID Issues," *Champion*, November 2004, p. 8.

72. *People &c. v. Robert Maldonado*, 1 No. 45 (NY Int. 40, 2002), emphasis in the original.

73. Robinson, *Crime Scene Photography*, p. 322.

74. John Horswell, "Crime Scene Photography," in *The Practice of Crime Scene Investigation*, ed. John Horswell. Boca Raton, FL: CRC Press, 2004, p. 126.

75. Aaron Doyle, *Arresting Images: Crime and Policing in Front of the Television Camera.* Toronto: University of Toronto Press, 2003, p. 72.

76. *People &c. v. Maldonado.*

77. Taylor, *Forensic Art and Illustration*, p. 549.

Glossary

age progression: The process of changing a person's photograph to make him or her look older.

anthropologist: A scientist who studies the culture and biology of human beings.

chain of custody: The process of documenting where criminal evidence has been and what has been done to it.

composite sketch: A drawing of a crime suspect's face based on a witness's description.

crime scene sketch: A rough sketch or diagram of the place a crime happened.

decompose: The process by which flesh breaks down, or rots.

defendant: The person in a court trial who has been accused of a crime.

defense attorney: The lawyer who defends the defendant against charges that he or she committed a crime.

document: To create records about a process.

expert witness: A witness in a trial who is considered an expert on a certain subject and can give professional opinions about it.

facial mapping: The use of several different methods to decide whether pictures of different faces are of the same person.

facial reconstruction: The art of recreating an unidentified person's face, usually using a skull.

forensic artist: A person who creates or adapts drawings, illustrations, sculptures, and graphics to help with a crime investigation.

fugitive: A criminal or suspect who is avoiding capture.

hearsay: Information that is not based on a witness's personal knowledge, but on something he or she heard someone else say.

hydrogen peroxide: A chemical combination of oxygen and hydrogen that is used to remove flesh from a skeleton.

image enhancement: The process of making changes to a photograph or image so that it is clearer and easier to see.

imagery analyst: A person who studies and compares photographs using knowledge of photography and science.

jury: The group of people who listen to both sides of a court trial and decide whether the defendant is guilty or innocent.

magnetic resonance imaging (MRI): The use of magnets and pulses of sound to create a precise, three-dimensional picture of an object.

pixel: The smallest unit of a digital picture or image.

prosecutor: The lawyer who tries to prove in court that a defendant is guilty.

superimpose: To lay one picture or image over the top of another.

three-dimensional: A picture or object that shows three dimensions: height, width, and depth.

tissue-depth marker: A marker, made of rubber, that is glued to a skull in various places during a facial reconstruction to show the artist how deep the flesh should be at each place.

two-dimensional: A picture or object that shows only two dimensions: height and width.

vellum: A sheet of see-through material many artists use to make drawings.

visual aid: Any item, drawing, or other visual object that helps to explain something.

For More Information

Books

Julie Adair King, *Photo Retouching & Restoration for Dummies*. New York: Wiley, 2002. This handbook explains, in words and pictures, how to edit digital images much the way a forensic image analyst might. It shows how computer software can remove glare from eyeglasses, mask elements in a picture, and perform other magic on an image. (Not everything presented in this book would be acceptable to do in a real investigation.)

Carrie Stewart Parks, *Secrets to Drawing Realistic Faces*. Cincinnati, OH: North Light Books, 2002. Written by an internationally known forensic artist and instructor, this book explains how to draw faces from hair to chin, using many of the same techniques forensic artists depend on.

Katherine M. Ramsland, *Forensic Science of CSI*. New York: Berkley, 2001. A forensic psychologist takes readers behind the scenes of the popular television show *CSI*, explaining the real basics of many crime-busting methods including age progression, forensic sculpting, and image modification.

DVD

History Channel, *Save Our History: Written in Bone*, DVD, History Channel, March 28, 2008, http://store.aetv.com/html/product/index.jhtml?id=115680.

Internet Sources

Brian Handwerk, "King Tut's New Face: Behind the Forensic Reconstruction," *National Geographic News*, May 11, 2005, http://news.nationalgeographic.com/news/2005/05/0511_050511_kingtutface.html.

Dina Temple-Raston, "FBI Unravels the Stories Skulls Tell," *National Public Radio*, January 28, 2008, www.npr.org/templates/story/story.php?storyId=18481926.

Web Sites

Doe Network (www.doenetwork.org). Doe Network is a national organization that helps law enforcement identify missing persons and unknown victims (John and Jane Does). Their Web site has examples of composite sketches and age progressions, links to more information, and ways for volunteers to get involved.

Forensic Art (www.forensicartist.com). Overviews of major kinds of forensic art can be found on this Web site, along with examples of composite sketches, facial reconstructions, and age progressions. There are also links to related projects and organizations.

Forensic Faces Institute (www.forensicart.org). Forensic Faces Institute has articles about different types of forensic art and links to many books, Web sites, and additional resources.

Index

Abramson, Leslie, *78*
Adobe Photoshop, 68
Age, 33, 47
Age progression
  America's Most Wanted and, 46–47, *48*
  computers and, 57–58
  creating, 47–48, 53–54
  described, 11
  effect of expressions, 47
  examples of, *50*, *55*
  facial features and, 54–55, 56
  lifestyle and, 48–49, 52
  surgical, 51
  three-dimensional, 45
Age regression, 49
Airplane hijacking case, 14, *14*
America's Most Wanted (television program), 46–47, *48*, 51
Anthropologists, 32–33
Arresting Images: Crime and Policing in Front of the Television Camera (Doyle), 87
ATM cameras, 63
Azarian, George, 65–66

Bace, Rebecca Gurley, 76, 80
Bach, Johann Sebastian, 30
Beijing, China, 66
Bender, Frank A., 45, *46*, 57
Bertillon, Alphonse, 9, *10*
Birth defects, 51, *52*
Blitzer, Herbert L.
  on extent of manipulation of photographs, 66, 68
  on importance of enhancing photographs, 63
  on layer control, 71
  on number of pixels per square inch, 71
  on using Adobe Photoshop, 68
Bodies, 29, 33–34
Body size, 36, 37

Carson, Eve Maria, 59, 63
Cell phones, 11
Chain of custody of evidence, 86–87
Children, 50–53, 56, 57
  See also Age progression
Chin, 53, 55
Clothing, 26–28, 32, 56
Composite sketches
  detail in, 15, 17, 21–22, 24, 28
  early, 8–10, 9
  as evidence, 10–11, 83–84, 86
  examples
    changes in facial hair, *25*
    compared to photograph, *82*
    Cooper, *14*
    Kaczynski, *27*
    suspect in murder of Biggie Smalls, 77, *77*
    use of shading, *22*
  facial features in, 23
  flawed but successful, 16–17
  leads and, 11
  nonfacial aspects, 26–28
  notes written on, 82–83
  percentage leading to suspect's capture, 16
  reliability, 10
  time factor, 20
  tips from, 15–16
Computer-generated facial reconstructions, *41*, 41–43
Computer-generated images, 35, *35*, *41*
Computers
  for age progression, 57–58
  drawing with, 20
  enhancing photographs, 61, 68–72, *70*
  facial mapping and, 74
Cooper, D. B., 14, *14*
Courts
  convictions of innocent defendants, 83
  evidence
    admissibility of, 85
    composite sketches as, 10–11, 83–84, 86

fingerprints and DNA as, 72, 84
hearsay, 85–86
paper as, 71–72
photographs as, 72–75, 86–87
videos as, 69
testimony
crime scene sketches and, *78*, 78–80
of forensic artists, 81–83
of forensic image experts, 72
models and, *80*
Cranial structure, 33, 34
Crime Scene Photography (Robinson), 72
Crime scene sketches, *78*, 78–80

Detecting Forgery: Forensic Investigation of Documents (Nickell), 71–72
Digital technology, 11, 68–72
See also Computers
DNA, 72, 84
Documents, examining, 71–72
Dostie, Paul, 31, 44
Doyle, Aaron, 87

Evidence
admissibility, 85
composite sketches as, 10–11, 83–84, 86
fingerprints and DNA as, 72, 84
hearsay, 85–86
paper as, 71–72
photographs as, 11, 62–63, 72–75, 86–87
used to determine characteristics of victims, 32–33
videos as, 69
Evison, Martin P., 39, 42–43
Expert witnesses, 81–83
Eyeglasses, *27*, 27–28
Eyes, 23, 53, 54–55

Faces
ability to remember, 8
effect of expressions on, 47, 54
measuring, 9
reference points, 53
unique identification markers, 24–25
Facial mapping, 74
Facial piercings, 24–25
Facial reconstructions
computer-generated, *41*, 41–43
Cooper case, 14
three-dimensional
age progression and, 45
creating, 30, *30*, 37–39
early, 30–31
two-dimensional, 39–40, *40*
Facial tissue measurements, 35–37, *36*
FBI Facial Identification Catalog, 21, 28
Fingerprints, 71, 72
Fisher, Barry A.J., 79
Forensic art
as calling, 16
documenting, 82–83
equipment, 20
purposes of, 81, 82, 89
Forensic artists
becoming, 18, 22–23
characteristics of, 13, 15
court testimony, 81–83
ego and, 39
as middle men, 32
number in U.S. (2008), 24
pressures on, 20
role, 11–12
Forensic image experts
becoming, 62
court testimony, 72
role, 60
Forgeries, 71–72

Gatliff, Betty Pat., 41–42, 44
Geberth, Vernon J., 39–40
Gender, 32–33, 36
Gibson, Lois
on details in composite sketches, 22, 28
on forensic art as calling, 16
on hair, 24
on hat size, 27–28
on notes taken while drawing, 83
on obvious facial features, 23
on pressures on forensic artists, 20
on success of flawed sketches, 16–17
on testimony of forensic artists, 81–82
on working with decomposing bodies, 33
A Guide to Forensic Testimony (Smith and Bace), 76

Hair
  age progression and, 55, 56
  example of changes in facial, *25*
  importance of, 24
Handheld laser scanners, 43
Hats, 27–28
Hearsay evidence, 85–86
Henderson, Charles Arlin, *55*
Hill, Ian, 19, 31, 33–34
His, Wilhelm, 30
Horswell, John, 87
Human remains, 29, 33–34

Image experts, 11
Imagery analysts, 73–75
Innocent defendants convicted, 83, 84
Innocent observers, 13

Jack the Ripper, 8, *9*
Jacobia, Jack
  on amount of manipulation of photographs, 66, 68
  on importance of enhancing photographs, 63
  on layer control, 71
  on number of pixels per square inch, 71
  on using Adobe Photoshop, 68
Juries, 76, 78–83, 86

Kaczynski, Theodore, *27*
Kansas bakery murder, *65*
Kennedy, John F., assassination of, 59

Las Vegas, NV casinos, 67, *67*
Laser scanners, 42, 43
Lifestyle and age progression, 48–49, 52
List, John, 45, 47, 57
Lute, Gwen, 66

Magnetic resonance imagining (MRI), 42
Mammoth Lake, California skull, 31, 33, 44
Mathematics and facial reconstructions, 41–42
McCrone, Brian, *88*
Memory
  of faces, 8
  photography and, 59–60
  of witnesses, 13, 21
Miller, Jerry, 84
Miller, Marilyn T., 72
Mouth, 53, 54, 55–56

NASA (National Aeronautics and Space Administration), 69
National Center for Missing and Exploited Children (NCMEC), 50–51
Neck, 26
New Orleans, Louisiana murder victim, *40*
New York Court of Appeals, 84, 87, 89
Nickell, Joe, 71–72
Nose, 23, 53

Ohio Historical Society, 49
Olympic Games, 66
Oxlee, Geoffrey
  on imagery analysis, 73, 74
  on importance of photographic evidence, 75
  on recognition of individuals in photographs, 73
  on surveillance camera photographs, 60–61

Photographs
  of crime scenes, 78–79
  enhancing
    amount of manipulation, 66, 68
    examples, 63, *64*, 65–66, *70*
    as only witness, 65
    steps, 61
  as evidence, 11, 62–63, 72–75, 86–87
  resolution of FBI scanners, 68
  See also Surveillance cameras
Pixels, 69–71, *70*
Plastic surgery, 51, *52*
The Practice of Crime Scene Investigation (Horswell), 87
Prince George's County, Maryland arson, 15–16

Race, 36
Ramsland, Katherine, 52
Recognition, 8, 20
Robinson, Edward M., 72, 86–87
Russ, John C., 54

Scars, 25
Security cameras. *See* Surveillance cameras

Shoulders, 26
Simpson, O.J., *88*
Sketch pads, 20
Skull, *34*
  creating three-dimensional facial reconstructions and, 30, *30*, 37–39
  fragility and facial reconstructions, 39–40, *40*
  increase in size of child's, 56
  information from, 33, 34
  uniqueness, 37
Smalls, Biggie, 77
Smith, Fred Chris, 76, 80
Steele, Lisa, 84
Sunglasses, *27*, 28
Surgical age progressions, 51
Surveillance cameras, *60*
  in Las Vegas casinos, 67, *67*
  number at Beijing Olympic Stadium (2008), 66
  as witnesses, 59–61, 65
  See also Photographs

Tattoos, 24–25
Taylor, Karen T.
  on age progression
    computers and, 57
    eyes, 54–55
    for missing children, 51
    teeth, 56
    training and, 53
    use of family photographs, 53
  on artistic ego, 39
  on computer-generated facial reconstructions, 43
  on effect of expressions on face, 47
  on forensic artist as middle man, 32
  on importance of cranial structure, 33
  on importance of identifying victims, 29
  on purposes of forensic art, 81, 82–83, 89
Teeth, 55–56
Tello, Johnny, *50*
Thomas, Richard B., *48*
Three-dimensional facial reconstructions
  age progression and, 45
  creating, 30, *30*, 37–39
  early, 30–31
Tiffin, Mary Worthington, 49
Tissue measurements, 35–37, *36*, 42
Touch pads and tablets, 20
Tutankhamun, 35, *35*
Two-dimensional facial reconstructions, 39–40, *40*
Two-dimensional image conversion, 68–69

Unabomber, *27*

Victims
  determining characteristics of, 32–33
  identifying bodies of, 29, 31
  percentage of unidentified homicide, 32
  as witnesses, 13, 15
Videos, 69
VISAR (Video Image Stabilization and Registration), 69
Visual aids, 21
Vogelsang, Janet, 80–81

Washington Times (newspaper), 15
Watts, Eugene Coral, *82*
Weber, Duane, 14
Weiss, Amber, 49
West, William, 9–10
Wilkinson, Caroline, 37
Witnesses
  expert, 81–83
  as innocent observers, 13
  interviewing, 19–21
  memory of, 13, 21
  reliability, 84–85
  surveillance cameras as, 59–61, 65
  types of, 19
  as victims, 13, 15
Woolhouse, Meg, 65
Wrinkles, 54

Picture Credits

Cover Image: © Digital Art/Corbis

Alfred Pasieka/Photo Researchers, Inc., 65

AP Images, 12, 20, 24, 36, 44, 47, 55, 58, 60, 62, 71, 72, 74, 76, 82

© Bettmann/Corbis, 8

© Digital Art/Corbis, 37

Mario Ruiz/Time Life Pictures/Getty Images, 42

© Mark Peterson/Corbis, 15

Michael Donne, University of Manchester/Photo Researchers, Inc., 27

Nancy J. Pierce/Photo Researchers, Inc., 33

Philippe Psaila/Photo Researchers, Inc., 30

Popperfoto/Getty Images, 7

Reuters/Landov, 22, 46

© Supreme Council for Antiquities/Handout/Reuters/Corbis, 31

UPI/Landov, 50

About the Author

Jenny MacKay is an editor of books and journal articles and the author of several nonfiction books for teens, including *Fingerprints and Impression Evidence*. She is currently pursuing her master of fine arts degree in creative writing. She lives with her husband and two children in northern Nevada, where she was born and raised.